BUILD IT
& THE CROWDS WILL COME

BILL BECK

75

SEVENTY-FIVE YEARS OF PUBLIC ASSEMBLY

BUILD IT
& THE CROWDS WILL COME

75
SEVENTY-FIVE YEARS OF PUBLIC ASSEMBLY

FROM THE AUTHOR

Writing a dedication is traditionally the last, and in some ways the hardest, task faced by the author. With *Build It and the Crowds Will Come*, the job of writing a dedication was made extraordinarily simple. The book is dedicated to the thousands of public assembly facility managers and their staffs, past and present, who make our attendance at conventions and trade shows, sporting events and live entertainment enjoyable, convenient, safe, and memorable.

Writing a book is always a collaborative process, and *Build It and the Crowds Will Come* is certainly no exception. Jack Zimmer, CAE, executive director of the International Association of Assembly Managers, Inc., was a gracious host during my visit to IAAM's Dallas headquarters. Don Hancock, who was IAAM's director of education, research, and development during the creation of this book, threw open the association's archives for my research and answered every question tossed his way. The IAAM History Committee read every word of the manuscript and made numerous constructive suggestions to strengthen the work.

Editors are a key element in the book-writing process. Maria Collis, my editor at Cherbo Publishing Group, is everything a writer asks an editor to be.

Finally, my wife, Betty, has been by my side, encouraging and supporting me through 15 years of the book-writing business. So this is her 25th book, too.

BILL BECK

PRESIDENT Jack C. Cherbo
EXECUTIVE VICE PRESIDENT Elaine Hoffman
EDITORIAL DIRECTOR Christina M. Beausang
MANAGING FEATURE EDITOR Margaret L. Martin
FEATURE EDITOR Maria Collis
CONTRIBUTING EDITOR Tina Rubin
SENIOR PROFILES EDITOR J. Kelley Younger
PROFILES EDITOR Diane M. Ver Steeg
SENIOR PROFILES WRITER Brian K. Mitchell
PROFILES WRITERS Barbara Beckley, Camilla Denton, Beth Mattson-Teig, Nancy Smith Seigle, Paul Sonnenburg, Diane M. Ver Steeg, and Stan Ziemba

SENIOR PROOFREADER Sylvia Emrich-Toma
ART DIRECTOR/DESIGNER Peri A. Holguin
PROFILES DESIGNER Mary C. Barnhill
PHOTO EDITOR Catherine A. Vandenberg
SALES ADMINISTRATOR Joan K. Baker
ACQUISITIONS ADMINISTRATOR Bonnie J. Aharoni
PRODUCTION SERVICES MANAGER Ellen T. Kettenbeil
ADMINISTRATIVE COORDINATOR Jahnna Biddle
EASTERN REGIONAL MANAGER Marcia Weiss
EASTERN DEVELOPMENT DIRECTOR Glen Edwards
SALES REPRESENTATIVE Front Row Marketing Services

Cherbo Publishing Group, Inc., Encino, Calif. 91316
© 2001 by Cherbo Publishing Group, Inc.
All rights reserved. Published 2001
Printed in the United States of America

Visit CPG's Web site at www.cherbopub.com.

Library of Congress Cataloging-in-Publication Data
Bill Beck
  A pictorial guide highlighting the history and development of public assembly facilities
  Library of Congress Card Number: 00-109442
  ISBN 1-882933-37-0

The information in this publication is the most recent available and has been carefully researched to ensure accuracy. Cherbo Publishing Group, Inc. cannot and does not guarantee the correctness of all the information provided and is not responsible for errors and omissions

V

PHOTO: © BETTMANN/CORBIS

IAAM INTERNATIONAL

BUILD IT
& THE CROWDS WILL COME

CONTENTS

CHAPTER 1   THE CHANGING ROLE OF THE PUBLIC FACILITIES MANAGER: A HISTORICAL OVERVIEW   2
A HISTORY OF THE BIRTH, GROWTH, AND ACCOMPLISHMENTS OF
THE INTERNATIONAL ASSOCIATION OF ASSEMBLY MANAGERS

CHAPTER 2   A VENUE MENU: PUBLIC ASSEMBLY FACILITIES   16
CONVENTION CENTERS, EXHIBITION HALLS, STADIUMS AND BALLPARKS,
THEATERS AND MUSIC HALLS, AND ARENAS AND AUDITORIUMS

CHAPTER 3   SOMETHING FOR EVERYONE: ENTERTAINMENT OPTIONS   36
SPORTING EVENTS, CONCERTS, PLAYS AND MUSICALS,
AUTO SHOWS, AUCTIONS, EXHIBITIONS, AND OTHER EVENTS

CHAPTER 4   THE DREAM MAKERS: ARCHITECTS AND PLANNERS   52
ARCHITECTS, ENGINEERS, AND THE DESIGN, DEVELOPMENT, AND
CONSTRUCTION OF PUBLIC FACILITIES

CHAPTER 5   BIG DEALS: CREATIVE FUNDING FOR PUBLIC FACILITIES   68
PREMIUM SEATING, LUXURY SUITES, NAMING RIGHTS, AND OTHER
OPTIONS THAT HELP PAY FOR NEW OR REMODELED VENUES

CHAPTER 6   INNOVATIVE THINKING: OPERATIONS AND EQUIPMENT   78
INVENTIONS AND INNOVATIONS THAT HAVE BEEN DRIVEN BY PUBLIC FACILITIES,
SUCH AS COMPUTERIZED TICKETING; WEBCASTING; ELECTRONIC SCOREBOARDS;
CONCESSIONS AND FOOD SERVICES; FLOORING, ROOFING, AND SEATING OPTIONS;
AND SPECIALIZED EQUIPMENT

CHAPTER 7   COMING ATTRACTIONS: THE FUTURE OF THE PUBLIC FACILITIES INDUSTRY   102
THE FUTURE OF PUBLIC FACILITIES, INCLUDING TECHNOLOGY TRENDS,
PRIVATE MANAGEMENT COMPANIES (CONTRACTED MANAGEMENT SERVICES),
BRANDING, CONVEYANCE OF SPORTS AND ENTERTAINMENT, AND
ENVIRONMENTAL CONSIDERATIONS

BIBLIOGRAPHY   116
INDEX   117

ASSOCIATION OF ASSEMBLY MANAGERS

SEVENTY-FIVE YEARS OF PUBLIC ASSEMBLY

75

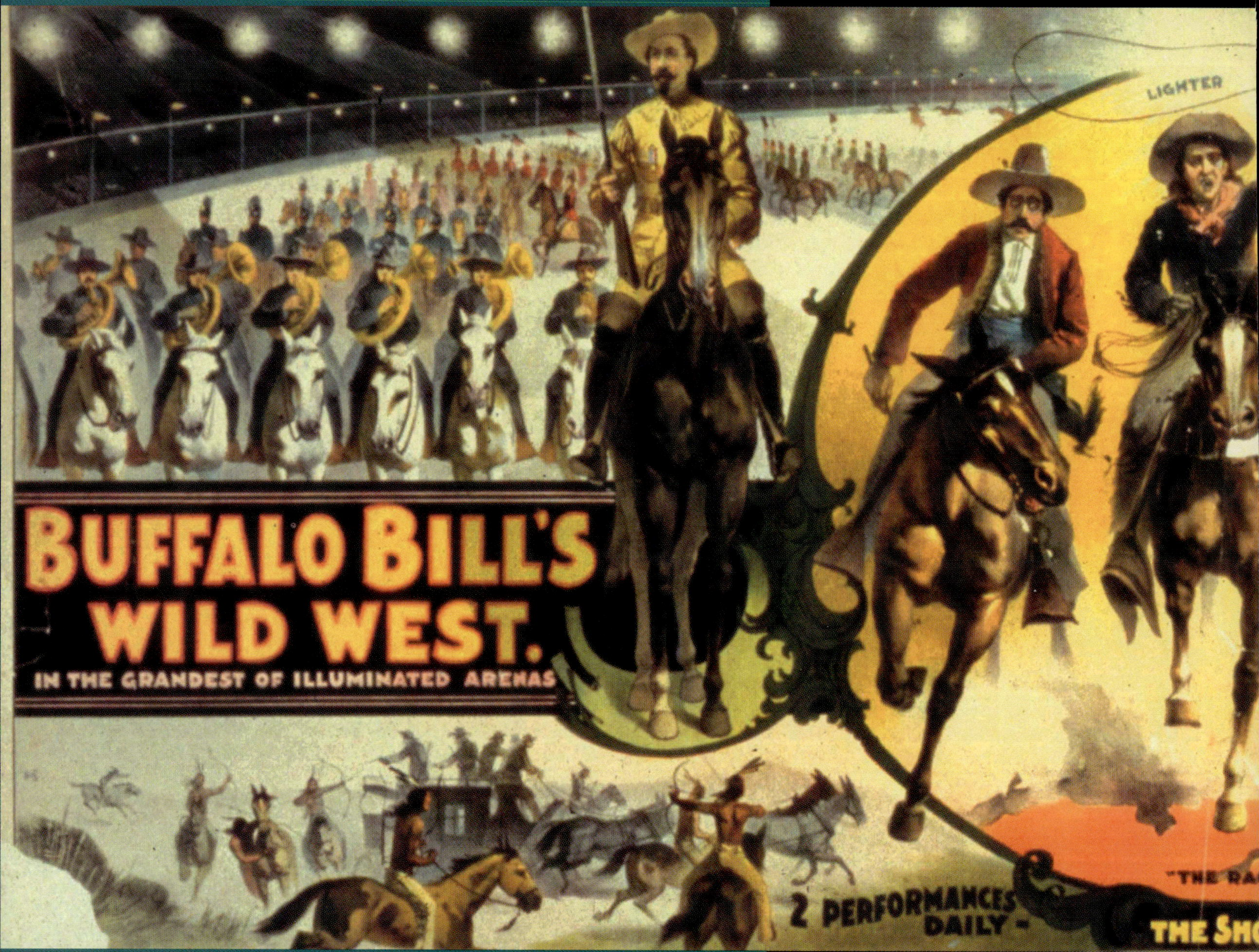

PHOTO: © HULTON GETTY

THAN DAY
AND CONGRESS OF
ROUGH RIDERS
OF THE WORLD
2 ELECTRIC PLANTS 250.000 CANDLE POWER
OF RACES"
OF SHOWS
RAIN OR SHINE

IAAM

CORPORATIONS & ORGANIZATIONS PROFILED

THE FOLLOWING COMPANIES AND ORGANIZATIONS HAVE MADE A VALUABLE CONTRIBUTION TO THE QUALITY OF THIS PUBLICATION. THE INTERNATIONAL ASSOCIATION OF ASSEMBLY MANAGERS GRATEFULLY ACKNOWLEDGES THEIR PARTICIPATION IN BUILD IT AND THE CROWDS WILL COME: SEVENTY-FIVE YEARS OF PUBLIC ASSEMBLY.

American Seating Company, 98

Anheuser-Busch Companies, Inc., 92–93

Clarin, A Division of Greenwich Industries, L.P., 94

Cumberland County Coliseum Complex, 34

Daktronics Inc., 90–91

Dallas Convention Center, 33

Geiger Engineers, 64

Global Spectrum, 114

Homasote Company, 66

Las Vegas Convention and Visitors Authority, 30–31

Miller Brewing Company, 28–29

R.I.C. Corp., 99

San Diego Convention Center Corporation, 35

Stephen C. O'Connell Center, University of Florida, 32

Sylvan Industries Inc., 97

Thornton-Tomasetti Engineers, A Division of The Thornton-Tomasetti Group Inc., 65

Ticketmaster, 100

Tickets.com, 95

White Way Sign Company, 96

World Wrestling Federation Entertainment, Inc., 48–50

INTERNATIONAL ASSOCIATION OF ASSEMBLY MANAGERS

Dear IAAM Member:

In 1998, under the leadership of President John Smith, IAAM started a process to plan and celebrate the Association's 75th anniversary as a professional association. A committee was formed and charged with creating a memorable and fitting tribute to commemorate this special anniversary milestone.

The committee was co-chaired by Peggy Daidakis and Michael Taormina, who set out to accomplish this task with the support of 3,000 IAAM members. Carol Wallace, who succeeded John Smith as IAAM president, continued the momentum of making this anniversary a reality as the 2000 IAAM Annual Conference in Nashville drew even closer. Meanwhile, Second Vice President Lionel Dubay and his Annual Conference Planning Committee went about its work to implement the plan.

Finally, the fruits of the collective labors put forth by IAAM staff, volunteers, and Association leadership culminated in Nashville with a number of events heralding the anniversary. What a memorable and fitting tribute we all shared in!

However, the work of the 75th Anniversary Committee did not end with the 2000 Annual Conference. The committee also wanted to provide our members with a lasting tribute to our industry and the leadership role of IAAM in public assembly facility management.

This book is the proud evidence of yet another project dedicated to our profession. With the faithful, hard work of the 75th Anniversary Committee, this book provides you with not only a history of IAAM, but an inside look at the public assembly facility industry.

I have stated on many occasions, as your current IAAM president, that I have a responsibility to be a caretaker for our Association and to provide, to the best of my abilities, not only a solid commitment to the health of our Association, but also to our industry.

As you read this enlightening book, take a moment to reflect upon the contributions of those who have preceded us, those individuals who have built the foundation on which our Association and industry stand. As we look forward to the next 75 years, each of us has an opportunity to make similar contributions to our industry. Seek out those opportunities for service.

Above all, let's continue to strive to make sure that IAAM's commitment as the acknowledged leader in public assembly facility management continues as strong in the next 75 years as it was in the preceding.

Enjoy the book!

Frank Poe

ONE
The Changing Role of the Public Facilities Manager: A Historical Overview

THE YEAR WAS 1924. AMERICA WAS ENJOYING ITS FIFTH YEAR OF RECORD PROSPERITY SINCE THE PEACE OF VERSAILLES ENDED WORLD WAR I IN 1919. AMERICA'S CITIES WERE BUSTLING,

and employment was at an all-time high. Millions of Americans were moving off the farms, which were experiencing postwar problems, to find a better life in the cities.

That movement into urban America was being aided by a veritable explosion of all-weather road construction. Henry Ford had introduced the automobile assembly line at Highland Park outside Detroit the decade before, and the Model T Ford had put the United States on the road in the early 1920s. At just over $600, the affordable Model T was showing up in the average middle-class American's garage. Customers also had dozens of makes and models to choose from in 1924, including Stutz, Marmon, Durant, Maxwell, Duesenberg, and Chrysler.

A second emerging social and technological phenomenon in 1924 was the rapid popularity of commercial radio. Station KDKA in Pittsburgh had become the first commercial radio station on the air in the United States in 1920. At that time, there were fewer than 2,000 radio sets in all of America. By 1924, every city and many towns in America boasted their own radio stations, broadcasting everything from sports to soap operas, from classical music to political conventions. By the end of the year, more than 2.5 million American homes had radio sets.

With its appetite for entertainment whetted by live radio broadcasts, and the possibilities for new mobility opened up by widespread automobile ownership, America embarked on a golden age of entertainment events. The Rose Bowl and Hollywood Bowl opened in California in 1923, and Colonel Jacob Ruppert opened Yankee Stadium in the Bronx that same year. The big doings on both coasts were followed in 1924 by the opening of Soldier Field in Chicago, the Forum in Montreal, and the Warner Theatre in Washington, D.C.

It was becoming obvious to those involved that managing auditoriums, arenas, and stadiums was a big business, getting bigger all the time.

ABOVE, LEFT TO RIGHT: IN OCTOBER 1924, FANS GATHER IN A NEW YORK CITY PARK TO LISTEN TO THE YANKEES GAME ON RADIO. • HENRY FORD STANDS PONDERING HIS FIRST INVENTION, THE QUADRICYCLE. BEHIND HIM IS THE 10 MILLIONTH MODEL T. • NEW YORK'S FIFTH AVENUE IS ALL ABUSTLE IN 1926. OPPOSITE: FIRST NAMED THE EARLE, WASHINGTON, D.C.'S WARNER THEATRE WAS PART OF A THRIVING DOWNTOWN CULTURAL SCENE IN THE 1930S. THE THEATER WAS RENOVATED IN 1992.

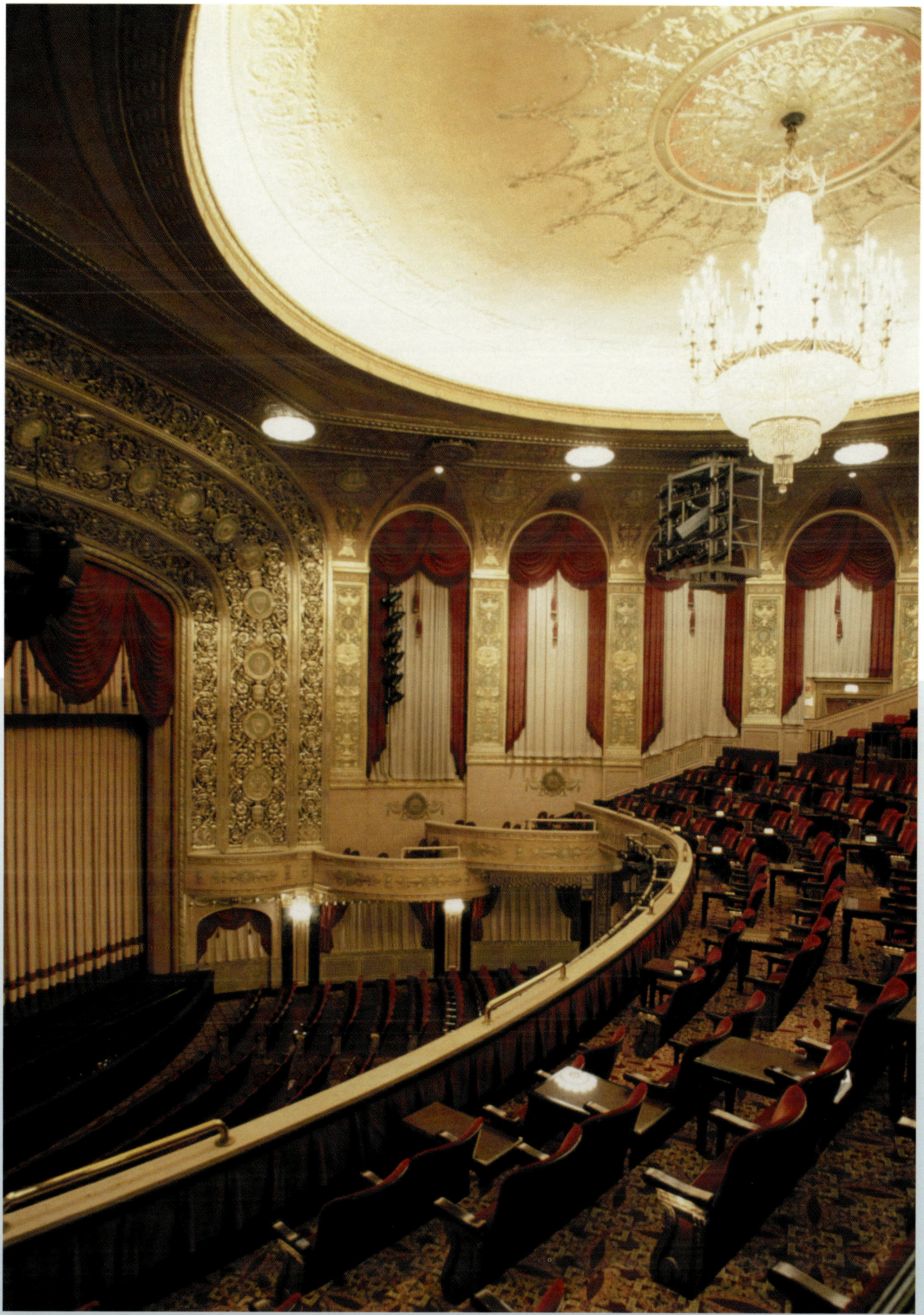

ONE

A Gathering of Visionaries

In early December 1924, auditorium managers Joseph G. Grieb of Milwaukee and Charles A. McElravy of Memphis put out a call for a meeting to discuss the increasingly important issues facing the industry. On December 27, 1924, six visionary building managers met in Cleveland to form the Auditorium Managers Association (AMA). Lincoln Dickey, who hosted the Cleveland meeting, served as first president. Grieb took up duties as secretary, and McElravy, Charles R. Hall of Chicago, William Bugge of Minneapolis, and Louis Shouse of Kansas City formed the organization's first board of directors. The association's first action was to establish a clearinghouse for sharing promotional ideas and disseminating information about member facilities to exhibitors nationwide.

All of the original directors managed auditoriums and arenas, then popular venues for the growing convention business. Automobile and interurban streetcar traffic had made it increasingly easy for convention-goers to travel to faraway cities for an annual or semiannual convention. In response, a number of cities established convention bureaus in the early 1920s to attract conventions and the dollars that came with them. The convention bureaus clamored for large exhibit halls for their patrons, and the result was a building boom in public assembly facilities.

The Memphis Municipal Auditorium McElravy managed was part of that boom. The New Orleans Municipal Auditorium was built from the same blueprints and, a year later, New York had a new Madison Square Garden. The Chicago Stadium opened in 1929.

Building slowed when the Great Depression hit, but resumed with federal Work Projects Administration (WPA) projects during the depression's waning years. The WPA helped build dozens of auditoriums, arenas, and coliseums around the country. All of these buildings needed managers, and all of these managers stood to benefit from sharing expertise with their peers—whether or not they realized it yet.

By the time the AMA held its 1934 conference, the membership had grown to about 30, including managers of some Canadian facilities, and the organization was renamed the International Association of Auditorium Managers (IAAM).

ABOVE: NEW YORK'S THIRD MADISON SQUARE GARDEN OPENED IN 1925 FOR BASKETBALL, HOCKEY, AND OTHER SPORTS. EARLIER VERSIONS HAD BEEN A CONVERTED RAILROAD STATION AND A BOXING ARENA. RIGHT: THIS DETAIL FROM A 1937 POSTCARD SHOWS PASADENA'S ROSE BOWL ON NEW YEAR'S DAY.

THE CHANGING ROLE OF THE PUBLIC FACILITIES MANAGER

The Beginnings of IAAM

Auditorium Managers Association members and spouses met at Chicago's 1931 conference to discuss issues such as the building boom. Renamed the International Association of Auditorium Managers in 1934, today's IAAM boasts a membership of over 3,000.

Charles A. McElravy was the fourth member of the original board of directors to take a turn as president of AMA, in 1929, before being named the organization's permanent secretary-treasurer in 1940.

Several issues concerned McElravy and the organization during the late 1920s and 1930s. As the number of arenas and auditoriums grew rapidly, facility managers became concerned that there would not be enough attractions to fill their seats on a regular basis. Aside from conventions, most public facilities were associated—at least by reputation—with boxing, dance marathons, roller derbies, and other rough forms of entertainment. Many facility managers had gotten their jobs through political connections, with no prior

The Ice Show Cometh

Arenas and auditoriums in the 1930s South often had no ice for touring ice shows. Years after booking the first *Holiday on Ice* in Memphis, Charles McElravy recalled how he improvised an ice rink at the Memphis Auditorium. McElravy hired contractors to lay pipe on the concrete floor of the auditorium's North Hall. They pumped brine through the pipes and then borrowed the Memphis Fire Department's fire hoses and pumpers to pump water over the chilled pipes. It was crude, but it worked. • Shown here is an ice-skating chorus line of the period performing in Berlin.

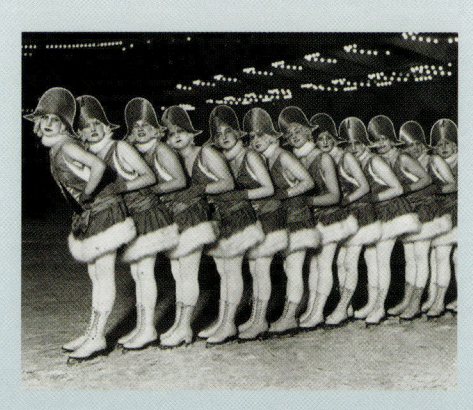

A Historical Overview

ONE

THE CHANGING ROLE OF THE PUBLIC FACILITIES MANAGER

OPPOSITE: CIRCUS ELEPHANTS HAVE DRAWN CROWDS TO ARENAS AND AUDITORIUMS SINCE LONG BEFORE THIS 1950S PHOTO. LEFT: AMONG THOSE AT THE MARCH 16, 1940, IAAM EXECUTIVE COMMITTEE MEETING WERE FOUNDING MEMBERS CHARLES A. MCELRAVY (FRONT ROW, FAR LEFT) AND JOSEPH GRIEB (FRONT ROW, FAR RIGHT). NEXT TO MCELRAVY IS EDNA CHRISTENSEN, IAAM'S FIRST FEMALE BOARD MEMBER.

experience and little job security. The buildings were often located away from the town center, and something was needed for them to gain regular mainstream audiences. Rodeos and circuses went over well, but more attractions were needed for the survival of the auditorium business.

In 1929, McElravy pushed for the formation of a committee to examine the relationship between auditorium managers and theatrical producers. The IAAM wanted to find out what producers needed to tour their shows from city to city and auditorium to auditorium. But many auditoriums did not have the lighting and staging adaptability needed for many theatrical productions, and differences in seating capacities of various venues made booking a circuit seem impractical. McElravy proposed creating a circuit for booking a "spectacular" tour. Spectaculars were just that: exuberant musical reviews with hundreds of performers in opulent costumes. And they were perfect for arenas and auditoriums with thousands of seats.

History would prove McElravy right: Spectaculars were a hit. One version of the spectacular that became a major boon to auditoriums and arenas was the touring ice show, which emerged in the late 1930s. Using popular Olympics champions such as Sonja Henie, the ice shows played to sold-out crowds across America, especially after several Hollywood movies, such as MGM's *Ice Follies of 1939*, popularized the shows.

Ice shows contributed greatly to the increased profitability of public facilities and prestige of their managers in the years before

THE IAAM PUBLIC ASSEMBLY FACILITY MANAGEMENT SCHOOL

In 1987, 53 students composed the first class at IAAM's Public Assembly Facility Management School (PAFMS) at the Oglebay Resort and Conference Center in Wheeling, West Virginia. The program was developed by the IAAM Foundation and the Professional Development Committee to provide professional instruction in facilities management and operations to practitioners in the field. • Students were, and still are, required to complete two intensive one-week sessions offered in consecutive years. Classes in 1987 covered such topics as personnel policies and management, budgeting, operating procedures, and public relations. The curriculum continues to evolve with the industry, and today's students also learn about computerization and privatization, among other subjects. • A unique program taught by top facilities management professionals, PAFMS has graduated more than 1,500 students. The school accepts 130 new students a year, with first preference given to IAAM members.

A HISTORICAL OVERVIEW

the Second World War. In 1942, *The Billboard* reported that auditoriums and arenas once almost completely dependent on sports events were now attributing 25 percent of their revenues to theatrical shows, and were all the better for it. These successes helped prove that large public facilities held great potential returns for producers willing to take their shows on the road.

That road seemed to extend further and further all the time. While there was only one AMA member who managed a facility west of Kansas City in 1925, by the early 1940s, IAAM had organized itself into districts that ranged from "eastern" to "western" to "Canadian." Regional districts made it easier for facility managers in different parts of the United States and Canada to meet and confer about local concerns. In addition, nonmanager employees of facilities could attend district meetings, and vendors often sponsored hospitality events at the meetings, giving both these groups a chance to mingle with IAAM members in the years before the organization instituted allied and associate memberships.

Still, due in part to the "managers only" admissions policy, the IAAM remained relatively small and close-knit through World War II and the 1950s. IAAM reported only 75 members in 1945, the year it formed its New Building Consulting Board (NBCB). The NBCB conducted surveys and offered advice that helped many communities plan new coliseums, auditoriums, and convention centers in the years of prosperity following World War II. Many of the new structures were built as war memorials.

Dixie Gregory, Charles McElravy's daughter, handled office chores for the IAAM from the 1940s to the 1960s. (She became the official Acting Secretary after her father's death in 1961.)

"The IAAM was the clearinghouse, the focal point for everything," Gregory told an interviewer in 1975. "If a manager had a problem, he would write Dad and say, 'See what you can get on this. Or so-and-so wants to know about such and such an attraction, or product, or operational problem.' And in the next month's edition of *Auditorium News*, we'd send it out."

Gregory recalled that times were tough until the organization began sponsoring trade shows in conjunction with the group's annual convention in 1953. "The association struggled for many years," she said. "Dues were only $65 a year then, so it was the trade show—there's always been an exhibit aspect to the convention—and the lovely affairs sponsored by various people that helped finance the IAAM conventions."

The annual trade show has continued to grow in size and

DON MYERS (CENTER) BECAME THE FIRST RECIPIENT OF IAAM'S MR. AUDITORIUM MANAGER AWARD AT THE 1953 ANNUAL CONFERENCE IN CHICAGO. FORMER IAAM PRESIDENTS C. W. VAN LOPIK (LEFT) AND CLARENCE HOFF ARE SHOWN PRESENTING THE AWARD.

importance in the years since Gregory retired and has become a vital point of contact for vendors of products and services and their facility manager clients, as well as an organization fund-raiser.

The 1950s witnessed strong growth in fairs and expositions around North America. Major fairs and expositions were opened in the 1950s in South Carolina,

THE CHANGING ROLE OF THE PUBLIC FACILITIES MANAGER

The IAAM Annual Conference & Trade Show

The IAAM has had a yearly conference since its founding in the mid-1920s. Conference attendees would meet to discuss such pertinent topics as technological advances, insurance, energy consumption, crowd management, and industry trends. • Only one booth was rented at IAAM's "First Educational Exposition" in 1953. But the IAAM trade show has grown to become an important aspect of the conference and a major source of income for the organization. • Mert Thayer (Chicago Amphitheater) gave birth to the idea, and Don Myers (Allen County War Memorial Coliseum, Fort Wayne, Indiana) nursed it from its infancy. Beginning in 1956, Myers produced the trade show and served as exhibits chairman for many years. By 1974, the show had grown so large that IAAM had to move its annual meeting from large hotels to convention centers. • The July 2000 IAAM Annual Conference and Trade Show boasted approximately 3,000 attendees and nearly 300 exhibits. The five-day program has come to be known throughout the industry as a premier opportunity for education, professional development, and networking for facility managers.

Georgia, Montana, Arkansas, Texas, Missouri, Florida, Kentucky, and Manitoba. Auditoriums and arenas built by the WPA in the 1930s, war memorials, and other assembly structures built especially for the fairs anchored many of these facilities.

The 1950s brought many changes to the circus industry, which had been a staple of the auditorium trade for years. In the 1950s, many of the smaller circuses went out of business. Then, in 1957, the Ringling Brothers and Barnum & Bailey Circus abandoned its half-century tradition of performing in tents for the more stable environment of arenas and auditoriums. This created a circus renaissance of sorts, which was good news for facilities managers. Circuses, the still-popular ice shows, and specialty attractions such as the Harlem Globetrotters played to packed audiences. These established crowd pleasers encouraged others: Jazz and blues artists and big-name stars such as Bob Hope began appearing on the arena circuit, many in appropriately large-scale productions. All this activity fostered another boom in the industry and in the IAAM.

IAAM's 1950s growth spurt included diversification. For the first time, the IAAM considered allowing the managers of open-air theaters and stadiums to join. Women had already made their appearance on the IAAM scene—at least as early as 1934, when Edna Christensen of Racine, Wisconsin, began her 11-year tenure on the board of directors. But it was those fabulous fifties (1958, to be exact) that saw IAAM's first female president, Winifred Corey of Buffalo, New York, take office. Diversity was to further define the organization in the 1960s.

In 1961, Charles McElravy, IAAM's guiding force for 37 years and the only surviving member of the organization's original board of directors, died in Memphis at the age of 82. His death marked the end of an era for IAAM.

Into the Modern Era

IAAM grew rapidly during the 1960s. Following McElravy's death, the board amended the constitution at the 1962 annual convention to put the organization on a more formal basis. Directors hired Charles R. Byrnes as IAAM's first full-time executive director, and Byrnes set up an office in Chicago.

Byrnes and IAAM's board embarked upon a major expansion for IAAM. They established a code of ethics, revamped the organization's newsletter, *Auditorium News*, to better serve as a communications tool within the industry, and established a personnel placement service for members.

In 1961, IAAM published its first industry statistical profile, which was updated in 1964 and 1969. In 1963, the organization launched a membership drive, which essentially tripled the number of members to 400 by 1968.

An important development for the organization came in 1963

A Historical Overview

when the board of directors established the Charles A. McElravy Award to honor outstanding members for "contribution to the IAAM and the profession of auditorium management." Another major landmark occurred in 1968 when IAAM established its scholarship program.

Rock 'n' roll audiences were a force to be reckoned with in the 1960s, and IAAM meetings grappled with issues of crowd control, no-show bands, and fans rushing the stage. IAAM launched its first annual management seminar in 1966.

The 1960s also witnessed a veritable explosion in construction of new multipurpose stadiums, arenas, auditoriums, and exhibit halls. In 1966, *Amusement Business* estimated that $800 million in new and renovation construction was either completed since 1964, under way, or on the drawing board. Sports, in particular, led the way in the construction boom. Many of the stadiums that have become famous to several generations of Americans date to the 1960s.

Much of this construction took place on college and university campuses. IAAM leaders recognized this period as a turning point for the industry and for their organization: Many IAAM members were now managers of stadiums, performing arts centers, and university facilities. IAAM responded to these members' concerns with special programming sessions, such as the first college and university building forum in 1968.

Regional districts also gained more of a voice in IAAM decision-making in the 1960s. District vice presidents were now included in the executive committee, and more frequent meetings were held, allowing IAAM activities to be planned and executed faster.

A BEACON TO PASSING FREEWAY AND AIRLINE TRAFFIC, LOS ANGELES'S $375 MILLION STAPLES CENTER IS BEAUTIFUL INSIDE, TOO, WITH HIGH-TECH FEATURES THAT INCLUDE AN IN-HOUSE STUDIO CAPABLE OF BROADCASTING HIGH-DEFINITION VIDEO LIVE VIA SATELLITE.

Growth in Professionalism

IAAM continued its growth toward professionalism during the 1970s and 1980s. Byrnes left the organization in 1972, and the directors hired the Chicago-based firm of Smith, Bucklin & Associates to manage IAAM. Smith, Bucklin ran the Association's affairs until 1978, when the directors selected another Chicago firm, P.M. Haeger and Associates, to handle day-to-day administrative duties.

Also in 1972, IAAM began forging some useful partnerships, becoming an affiliate of the Convention Liaison Committee, a powerful eight-member organization. The next year, IAAM's Performing Arts Committee began working with the National Endowment for the Arts (NEA). These activities and others were geared toward increasing professionalism among the membership—a membership that continued to grow.

IAAM capitalized on its 1960s statistical data reports by publishing its first industry profile survey in 1974, and expanding the survey in 1979. In 1975, IAAM celebrated its golden anniversary at an annual

THE CHANGING ROLE OF THE PUBLIC FACILITIES MANAGER

conference held jointly in Detroit, Michigan, and Windsor, Ontario.

Canadian members had always been active in IAAM. But the organization remained almost entirely North American until the early 1970s, when one intrepid Australian, John Elden of Melbourne, began to attend IAAM conferences regularly. Then, in 1975, members of the European Association of Arena and Auditorium Managers (EAAAM) made a three-week tour of IAAM facilities in the United States. One of the tour's leaders, Heinz Warneke of Berlin, became IAAM's first European member. Other delegations followed, and IAAM representatives began to reciprocate, attending conferences held by sister associations in Europe, Australia, New Zealand, and other countries.

By this time, public assembly facility managers were entering the field with academic degrees that didn't even exist at the time of IAAM's founding, degrees in subjects such as theater arts and business administration.

Considering the general increase in education level of IAAM members in the 1970s, perhaps it is not surprising that professional continuing education came into its own during this decade. IAAM hosted its first Professional Auditorium Management Symposium at the University of Illinois in Champaign in 1972, and an IAAM task force began studying the creation of a certification program in 1973. By 1976, IAAM had introduced seminars for specific facility management groups and established a certified facilities executive (CFE) program. Today, individuals holding CFE certification from IAAM command great respect within the public assembly facilities industry.

In line with its emphasis on continuing education, IAAM established the IAAM Foundation in 1981. With its mission to raise funds to support the public assembly facility profession in a variety of programs, including research, professional development, and education, the foundation quickly moved to create the IAAM Executive Development Series (EDS). The first EDS seminar was held at district meetings beginning in January 1983.

Over the years, the IAAM Foundation has undertaken a number of association initiatives,

THE BURGEONING PUBLIC ASSEMBLY INDUSTRY IS STRENGTHENED BY NEW AND EXPANDED SPORTS AND ENTERTAINMENT FACILITIES. SEATTLE'S SAFECO FIELD (SHOWN ABOVE UNDER CONSTRUCTION) OPENED IN JULY 1999. MILWAUKEE'S $400 MILLION MILLER PARK (RENDERING SHOWN LEFT) IS SCHEDULED TO OPEN IN APRIL 2001. BOTH BALLPARKS SPORT RETRACTABLE ROOFS AND REAL GRASS.

A HISTORICAL OVERVIEW

covering a broad spectrum of issues important to the industry. Prominent among these was the first annual Crowd Management Seminar, which followed shortly after the formation of EDS and was cosponsored by the University of Louisville and the Center for the Study of Crowd and Spectator Behavior. An annotated bibliography on crowd management grew from this seminar as well.

The foundation funded both a revised industry profile survey and a resource bank of publications and other materials pertaining to the industry. The organization also provided hands-on Internet training for members and helped fund the Society for the Preservation of Professional Touring Entertainment History's "Plan for a Living Archive" and the IAAM College Internship Program. In the late 1980s, the IAAM Foundation joined the National Highway Traffic Safety Administration's Techniques for Effective Alcohol Management (TEAM) coalition to promote responsible alcohol use in public assembly facilities.

In 1987, the foundation, together with IAAM's Professional Development Committee, opened the now internationally renowned IAAM Public Assembly Facility Management School.

The year 1982 was significant in that IAAM opened its doors beyond the titular heads of public assembly facilities. New categories of membership were created for professionals in other prominent management and administrative positions, as well as for retirees and vendors of products and services.

IAAM inaugurated a new long-range planning committee in 1984 and began publishing *IAAM News*, a new monthly newsletter. The association created a job placement service in 1985 and introduced *Facility Manager*, a quarterly color publication devoted to in-depth coverage of issues facing the membership.

After 15 years of management by association management firms in Chicago, IAAM moved back to a self-management system in 1987 when it again hired a full-time executive director. The next year, IAAM recorded a double milestone. It signed up its 1,600th member and relocated its headquarters to White Plains, New York.

IAAM's scope was increasingly global in focus. In early 1989, IAAM's president participated in meetings with his counterparts in England and France and laid the groundwork for industry meetings in Australia late in 1989 and in Berlin in 1990.

John Swinburn came aboard as executive director in 1989, and IAAM soon after moved to the

BELOW: A STATE-OF-THE-ART SPORTS VENUE SUCH AS INDIANAPOLIS'S CONSECO FIELDHOUSE REQUIRES A COMPLEX SET OF FINANCIAL, PUBLIC RELATIONS, OPERATIONS, AND ADMINISTRATIVE SKILLS TO MANAGE. OPPOSITE: SPECTATORS FILL THE TORONTO SKYDOME'S 60,000 SEATS, A SIGN THAT, MORE THAN EVER, PEOPLE ENJOY GATHERING TO EXPERIENCE LIVE ENTERTAINMENT.

THE CHANGING ROLE OF THE PUBLIC FACILITIES MANAGER

13

A Historical Overview

THE CHANGING ROLE OF THE PUBLIC FACILITIES MANAGER

LEFT: IAAM'S NEW COPPELL, TEXAS, HEADQUARTERS FEATURES A CYLINDRICAL GLASS CONFERENCE CENTER FOR BOARD MEETINGS, CONFERENCES, AND SEMINARS; OFFICES FOR STAFF; AND 20,000 SQUARE FEET OF SPACE FOR FUTURE GROWTH. OPPOSITE: SUNLIGHT STREAMS INTO A CONCOURSE AT TOKYO'S MULTIPURPOSE SAITAMA SUPER ARENA.

Dallas–Fort Worth area in Texas. The association added a professional development manager to the staff in 1991 and brought many contracted functions in-house in the mid-1990s when it created staff positions for management of meetings and trade shows. IAAM launched *Crowd Management*, a new quarterly devoted to safety and security issues, in 1994. *Facility Manager* increased its frequency from quarterly to bimonthly.

IAAM Today

Membership topped 2,300 in 1995 when IAAM opened the membership to students and created an at-large board of directors seat for university-based facility managers. In 1996, IAAM changed its name, but not its initials or logo. There were now relatively few members with the professional title "auditorium manager." The new name, "International Association of Assembly Managers," more accurately reflected the organization's diversity.

Today's IAAM members manage amphitheaters, arenas, auditoriums, convention centers and exhibit halls, performing arts venues, racetracks, stadiums, and university complexes. They hail from the worlds of entertainment, sports, conventions, trade shows, and tourism/hospitality. More than three-quarters of them are CEOs and/or general managers of public assembly facilities.

Recognizing the diversity of its membership, IAAM continues to develop and host comprehensive periodic specialty meetings, such as the Arena Management Conference, the International Convention Center Conference, the Performing Arts Facility Administrators Seminar, and the International Crowd Management Conference.

As it prepared to celebrate its 75th anniversary at the turn of the millennium, IAAM had big plans for the future. A newly implemented strategic plan served as the launching pad for several new initiatives, including a renewed focus on university facility management development, efforts to enhance the public perception of IAAM, and an expansion of professional development opportunities.

Together with the EAAAM and the Venue Management Association (VMA), IAAM launched the World Council for Venue Management (WCVM) in January 1997. Currently, nine associations representing more than 5,000 venue managers in over 1,600 facilities across the globe compose the WCVM, whose mission is to be a "globalized information clearinghouse for the public assembly facility management industry."

In April 2000, the IAAM staff moved into its new, 40,000-square-foot world headquarters in Coppell, Texas. The elegant glass structure was designed so that managers of state-of-the-art assembly buildings would feel right at home when attending IAAM meetings and events. Near Dallas–Fort Worth International Airport, a major interstate highway, and a new business park, the building's location in Dallas County's "hottest corridor" also reflects IAAM's progress and aspirations for future growth.

Today's IAAM is the world's largest professional association of its kind. With a full-time staff of 23, a 17-member board of directors, and more than 3,000 members in more than 150 countries, IAAM has come a long way from its founding in Cleveland by six forward-thinking auditorium managers just over 75 years ago.

A HISTORICAL OVERVIEW

TWO

A VENUE MENU:
PUBLIC ASSEMBLY FACILITIES

IN MANY WAYS, AUDITORIUMS, ARENAS, STADIUMS, ASSEMBLY HALLS, AND OTHER ENTERTAINMENT VENUES HAVE DEFINED AMERICAN POPULAR CULTURE IN THE 20TH CENTURY.

ABOVE, LEFT TO RIGHT: ELEANOR ROOSEVELT RESPONDS TO CHEERS AT THE 1960 DEMOCRATIC NATIONAL CONVENTION AT LOS ANGELES'S SPORTS ARENA. • THE CROWN COLISEUM AT THE CUMBERLAND COUNTY COLISEUM COMPLEX IN FAYETTEVILLE, NORTH CAROLINA, HOSTS MANY POPULAR EVENTS, SUCH AS THE HARPER AND MORGAN RODEO (CENTER) AND HOME GAMES OF THE CENTRAL HOCKEY LEAGUE'S FAYETTEVILLE FORCE (RIGHT). OPPOSITE: THE LOS ANGELES COLISEUM WAS THE SITE OF THE 1932 OLYMPICS, WHERE LAURI LEHTINEN OF FINLAND (SHOWN LEADING) SET A NEW RECORD FOR THE 5,000-METER RUN.

Who has not watched their favorite sports team do battle on the field of play? How many people in the developed world have not attended a play, symphony, popular music concert, or other live entertainment? What portion of the U.S. population has not journeyed to Los Angeles, Chicago, New York, or any state capital to spend a few days at a convention, professional meeting, or political rally? Practically everyone at some time in his or her life takes the opportunity to visit a public assembly facility. In the latter half of the 20th century, television has made those facilities cultural icons.

Society takes sports and entertainment seriously. Americans alone spend billions of dollars each year attending sporting and entertainment events. But few people are able to appreciate the complex choreography that goes into making an entertainment venue a safe, enjoyable, hassle-free environment for spectators.

You Can't Tell Your Arena Without a Scorecard

The term "public assembly facility," or "PAF" for short, embraces arenas, auditoriums, stadiums, convention centers, theaters, and other types of venues. All of them are specially designed facilities where the general public can come together in comfort and safety to watch athletic events and entertainment performances or to participate in conventions or conferences. Each of them has specific defining traits. To paraphrase Gertrude Stein, an arena is an arena is an arena. And an auditorium is an auditorium is an auditorium.

Colosseum vs. Coliseum

The progenitor of all public assembly facilities in the world today is the Roman Colosseum, an open-air stadium built two millennia ago by the Roman emperors to showcase circuses, athletic events, and gladiatorial contests. The Los

17

TWO

Angeles Memorial Coliseum—with its Americanized spelling—opened in October 1923 and hosted the 1932 and 1984 Summer Olympics. The Coliseum has since been home at various times to the Los Angeles Dodgers of baseball's National League (NL), the Los Angeles Rams and Raiders of the National Football League (NFL), and the University of Southern California Trojans. The Coliseum was designated a historical landmark in 1984. An open-air stadium with a seating capacity of 88,000, the Coliseum has architectural roots in its Roman predecessor.

But the word "coliseum" has also frequently been used during the 20th century to describe many exhibition halls, arenas, and stadiums throughout the United States. The New York Coliseum, for example, is really an exhibition hall.

The Will Rogers Coliseum in Fort Worth sports a domed ceiling supported by arched trusses to create unobstructed views. It was the brainchild of millionaire Amon G. Carter and a group of Fort Worth businessmen, who felt that Fort Worth should have some part of the 1936 Texas Centennial celebration to be held in neighboring Dallas. A request to the federal Public Works Administration (PWA) for an auditorium and coliseum was turned down, but Carter was able to get funding from President Franklin D. Roosevelt in 1935. Although it was not ready in time for the centennial, the Will Rogers Coliseum has more than earned its keep in ensuing years, hosting everything from conventions to horse shows to religious revivals.

Arenas, Auditoriums, Theaters, and Amphitheaters

An arena is a facility with a flat floor, usually equipped with anywhere from 8,000 to 22,000 seats. The arena is typically configured in an oval shape, and the seating is contained on one or more tiers. Arenas generally host events such as basketball games, hockey games, circuses, ice shows, indoor soccer, and arena football.

An auditorium is similar to an arena in that it has a flat floor, is built in an oval, and often has a horseshoe-shaped seating layout that focuses the line-of-sight on the floor. Auditoriums are generally much smaller than arenas, however. Many auditoriums, which were very popular with U.S. municipal planners from the 1920s to the 1940s, have a stage at one end of the facility for concert and theatrical performances. These auditoriums typically hosted high school and college

ABOVE: CONSTRUCTION ON THE ROMAN COLOSSEUM BEGAN IN A.D. 70 AND WAS COMPLETED FIVE YEARS LATER, RESULTING IN A 45,000- TO 50,000-SEAT STADIUM THAT IS STILL IMPOSING AFTER NEARLY 2,000 YEARS. RIGHT: BUILT ENTIRELY OF MARBLE ON THE SITE OF A STONE STADIUM DATED TO 330 B.C., ATHENS'S OLYMPIC STADIUM HOSTED THE FIRST MODERN OLYMPIC GAMES IN 1896.

A Venue Menu

THE RODEO GRAND ENTRY GIVES PARTICIPANTS IN THE SOUTHWESTERN EXPOSITION AND LIVESTOCK SHOW IN FORT WORTH, TEXAS, A CHANCE TO STRUT THEIR STUFF. EACH YEAR, THE SHOW DRAWS 800,000 PEOPLE OVER TWO WEEKS TO THE WILL ROGERS COLISEUM.

basketball games, circuses, or small trade shows. Since the mid-20th century, most municipalities have chosen to replace the traditional auditorium with single-use theaters, arenas, and exhibition halls.

The theater is perhaps the oldest of the American public assembly facilities. Theaters were brought to the New World from England and France, and the theater was popular in colonial America. In the late 19th and early 20th centuries, every major city in the United States boasted of its downtown theaters or "opera houses," hosting a wide variety of touring musical and dramatic ensembles.

Theaters generally contain 300 to 3,500 fixed seats, and temporary seating can be added to increase the house capacity. A theater includes a permanent stage, with seating arranged on a sloped floor in front

WORLD'S LARGEST

The largest football stadium in use in the world today was built for the sport Americans know as soccer. Located in the famed Brazilian port city of Rio de Janeiro, Maracanã Stadium can seat 155,000 soccer fans. The stadium was erected in 1950 for the IV World Cup of Football. Although Brazil ultimately lost the cup to Uruguay, a world record for attendance was set during the final game of that contest. Nearly 200,000 fans (199,854 to be exact), many of whom watched from standing terraces, witnessed Brazil's surprise defeat with a score of 1–2. • According to Guinness, the largest stadium ever built was for the sport of gymnastics. The Strahov Stadium in Prague, Czech Republic, opened in 1934 to accommodate 240,000 spectators in the stands and 40,000 athletes on the field. The stadium was used for massive synchronized exercise performances by members of Sokol, the nationalist Czech physical fitness movement founded in 1862. While Sokol is still alive and well, it can no longer fill the huge facility, and officials are considering building a smaller soccer stadium within the confines of the original 15-acre structure.

PUBLIC ASSEMBLY FACILITIES

TWO

20

A Venue Menu

PHOTOS: THIS PAGE, © HULTON-DEUTSCH COLLECTION/CORBIS; FACING PAGE, © NIK WHEELER/CORBIS

LEFT: BUILT IN 1928 AND STILL PACKING IN THE CROWDS, LOS ANGELES'S HOLLYWOOD BOWL IS ONE OF THE NATION'S MOST FAMOUS AMPHITHEATERS. OPPOSITE: THE FIRST METROPOLITAN OPERA HOUSE HAD BOXES ON EVERY LEVEL TO PLEASE SOCIAL-MINDED NEW YORKERS. IT SERVED FROM 1883 UNTIL 1966, WHEN THE NEW "MET" OPENED AS PART OF LINCOLN CENTER.

of and to the sides of the stage. A loft above the stage allows for the quick change of scenery for dramatic productions. Many theaters also include acoustic shells and orchestra pits.

The amphitheater is one of the more popular trends in modern entertainment venue construction. Fully half of the amphitheaters in existence today have been developed and built during the past two decades.

Newer amphitheaters often accommodate an audience of 15,000 to 20,000 people. The amphitheater is essentially an outdoor theater with a permanent roof but no walls. Roughly 40 percent of the audience is seated in fixed, covered seats; the remainder of the audience is seated on a grassy slope under the stars. Most amphitheaters are seasonal in character, although an increasing number of the more recent venues include semipermanent side enclosures that allow the amphitheater to be used during the colder months.

STADIUMS AND BALLPARKS

Perhaps the best-known entertainment venue in America is the stadium or ballpark. Stadiums have been built for most of the 20th century for the viewing of baseball and football games, with venues such as Yankee Stadium, Wrigley Field, and the Yale Bowl dating to the 1910s and 1920s.

A ballpark is, in fact, a type of stadium. Both stadiums and ballparks are generally bigger than arenas.

Professional and college football stadiums are characterized by

BUILDING A NEW CONCERT HALL

Performing arts centers often stretch the possibilities of public assembly facilities within a standard design. Australia's Sydney Opera House, for example, is a landmark recognized the world over. Los Angeles's planned Walt Disney Concert Hall, already the recipient of an honor award from *Progressive Architecture Magazine*, will be no less eye-popping, looking more like a giant steel sculpture than a highly functional building. The hall will be an addition to the downtown Performing Arts Center of Los Angeles County and is scheduled to become the new home of the Los Angeles Philharmonic Orchestra in 2003. The 2,250-seat auditorium and two smaller outdoor amphitheaters were designed to strict acoustic calculations. Architect Frank Gehry solicited the input of performing artists, contractors, and the Walt Disney family (who provided start-up money and additional funds later on) to make sure the hall's performance, rehearsal, and public spaces meet the needs of both artists and community. According to project supporters, the Performing Arts Center, including the Walt Disney Concert Hall, will create a vibrant north end to a cultural/entertainment corridor spanning the downtown area southward to the STAPLES Center.

PUBLIC ASSEMBLY FACILITIES

TWO

rectangular or oval configurations that seat anywhere from 60,000 to more than 100,000 fans. The rectangular football field is 120 yards long, including end zones, allowing for ample stadium seating. National Football League stadiums typically seat between 60,000 and 85,000, and the NFL will not site a Super Bowl game at a stadium that seats less than 70,000 people.

The typical ballpark, built for baseball, features a boomerang-shaped seating arrangement. In most major league baseball parks, the best seating is behind home plate and along the right field and left field lines; center field bleacher seating is as much as 450 feet from the center of action at home plate. Add to this the fact that more baseball games are played in a given season than football games—meaning less attendance per game—and it is understandable that ballparks, while still sizable, tend to have fewer seats than football stadiums: between 40,000 and 50,000.

A stadium variation that enjoyed some popularity with major league team owners in the last third of the 20th century is the domed stadium. The Astrodome, the United States' first domed stadium, opened in Houston, Texas, in 1965. Domed stadiums have typically been multipurpose facilities, often hosting a community's professional baseball and football teams. Cold-weather communities, such as Minneapolis, Toronto, and Montreal, have been big fans of domed stadiums, particularly for early-spring baseball games. Some domed stadiums, such as the Astrodome in Houston and Olympic Stadium in Montreal, have fixed roofs. Others, such as the Hubert H. Humphrey Metrodome in Minneapolis and the RCA Dome in Indianapolis, have a free-form fabric roof supported by a complex internal air pressure system.

Domed stadiums proved their versatility in the 1990s, increasingly serving as venues for major events such as the annual National Collegiate Athletic Association's (NCAA) men's and women's basketball tournaments and the quadrennial conventions of the major political parties. Ironically, the domed stadium configuration has fallen out of favor with major league baseball owners, the group that initially popularized them. The ballparks built during the latter half of the 1990s—the Ballpark in Arlington, Jacobs Field in Cleveland, Oriole Park at Camden Yards in Baltimore, and Coors Field in Denver—were all conventional ballparks of a form that fans from the heyday of Babe Ruth and Connie Mack would likely recognize.

From Exhibit Halls to Convention Centers

People utilize public assembly facilities to participate in events, too. There is a whole host of gathering places that cater to the convention and conference trade.

The exhibit hall is typically a one-story building with a flat floor and between 50,000 and one million square feet of exhibit space.

BELOW: NICKNAMED THE FRIENDLY CONFINES, WRIGLEY FIELD IN CHICAGO IS THE SECOND OLDEST U. S. MAJOR LEAGUE BALLPARK, BUILT IN 1914, JUST TWO YEARS AFTER BOSTON'S FENWAY PARK. OPPOSITE: MONTREAL'S 1976 OLYMPIC STADIUM HAS A FIXED, SUSPENDED KEVLAR ROOF.

Exhibit halls in the United States are generally built as part of a convention center and usually contain more exhibition space than the largest hotel in the community. European and Canadian exhibit halls are traditionally separate from other meeting facilities, and Europeans call this type of structure a "trade fair."

When an exhibit hall is sited in the middle of a city, its floor space is limited by how many blocks of prime real estate can be closed off to accommodate it. For that reason, exhibit halls are most often located

A Venue Menu

on the fringe of the urban core, next to a body of water or a railroad line.

The convention center contains one or more exhibit halls plus a large number of multipurpose rooms for meetings. Most convention centers contain a fully equipped industrial kitchen and separate banquet halls.

The convention center in Europe is frequently called a "congress center," and because it often hosts diplomatic meetings, the congress center is usually equipped with a fixed-seat theater. Separated in years past from trade fair buildings, many congress centers are now adding exhibit halls or being built together with them as European associations recognize the financial advantages of joining the two functions.

In the United States, conference centers are designed to host smaller meetings and typically provide sleeping rooms as well as state-of-the-art meeting facilities. Some cities are also financing and operating conference center facilities, but without the hotel component. Some conference centers are located in self-contained resort facilities. In general, the level of planning and technical services in a conference center is higher than that available in a convention center.

The merchandise mart is an offshoot of the exhibit hall and is generally dedicated to a specific industry. The merchandise mart is particularly popular in the textile and retail apparel trade. Located in a mid- to high-rise building, it typically consists of offices, a number of permanent showrooms, and 30,000 to 50,000 square feet of exhibit space catering to the buyers in that particular industry. While merchandise marts are not typical public assembly facilities, their presence or absence does have an impact on the amount of business channeled to other local facilities, such as convention centers and exhibit halls.

The trade center is generally located in a downtown, special-purpose office building that caters to companies and institutions doing international trade business. It is not a public assembly facility in the sense meant here, either. But since trade centers in some parts of the world, such as Southeast Asia, often display their country's primary exports, the differences between merchandise marts, trade centers, and trade shows are noted here for reference.

BIG BUSINESS

In the United States, a society that understands business as well as any society on earth, public assembly facilities are big business.

Consider the following: Per the National Endowment for the Arts, Americans spent $10.4 billion in 1998 to see live shows, a total that exceeds what they spent to see movies or sports.

TWO

The International Association of Assembly Managers (IAAM) reports that there are 730 theaters and auditoriums in the United States that host live shows. In 1998, attendance at those venues was estimated at more that 112.5 million people.

In addition, the 576 arenas in the United States drew more than 217 million people to events at their facilities in 1998 alone. The total direct operating income for the nation's 576 arenas that year was more than $1.1 billion.

As for stadiums and ballparks, the IAAM lists a total of 460 in the United States in 1998, 35 with professional sports franchises and 425 affiliated with universities or other entities.

ABOVE: PENN STATE'S BEAVER STADIUM, HOME OF THE NITTANY LIONS (SHOWN HERE BATTLING THE NORTHWESTERN WILDCATS), CAN SEAT CLOSE TO 100,000 FANS. BELOW: BALTIMORE'S 1992 ORIOLE PARK AT CAMDEN YARDS IS REMINISCENT OF EARLY 20TH-CENTURY BALLPARKS.

According to PriceWaterhouseCoopers, the Big Five accounting firm that has extensively studied the economics of public assembly facilities in America, professional football, basketball, and hockey operate at an average capacity factor of above 80 percent, while major league baseball's capacity factor of 43 percent is offset somewhat by having far more games in a typical season than its counterparts in professional sports. At an average ticket price of $40.10 for the National Basketball Association (NBA) and $37.50 for the National Football League (NFL), a professional football franchise, for example, can take in more than $2 million for a sold-out game on any given Sunday.

Then there are the convention centers and exhibit halls. The 319 such facilities in the United States are the champions when it comes

A VENUE MENU

to utilization, with an average facility hosting events 316 days of each year. All told, exhibit space in the United States totals more than 63.4 million square feet, according to *Tradeshow Week's 1999 Major Exhibit Hall Directory.*

According to the Professional Convention Management Association (PCMA), the convention, exposition, and meetings industry generates direct spending of more than $80 billion a year, supporting more than 1.5 million jobs and producing an estimated $12 billion of estimated tax revenue a year.

AN ECONOMIC ENGINE

Humankind's love affair with entertainment and sports has been a constant throughout history. That love affair is likely to continue well into the 21st century, a fact that is not lost on public assembly facility planners and managers.

The continuing popularity of entertainment, trade shows, sporting events, and exhibits is an economic engine that continues to drive major construction projects at the dawn of the 21st century. New concert venues in the United States, including arenas, auditoriums, and university and minor league sports stadiums that can double as concert and touring show venues, will account for more than $4 billion in construction funding between 1997 and 2002. There are 77 new construction or renovation projects either complete or on the drawing boards in the United States.

Business is also booming in the convention center and exhibit hall business. Between August 1998 and August 1999, more than one million square feet of new and expanded exhibit space opened in North America. Between 1999 and 2004, an additional 14.2 million square feet of new and expanded exhibition space is scheduled to open in North America. A total of 87 projects represents a 29 percent increase in projected exhibit space from mid-1998, an indication that municipalities and private investors are gaining increasing confidence in the market's ability to absorb new space.

Professional sports venues are also in an expansion mode. In November 1999, the NBA's Los Angeles Lakers opened their championship 1999–2000 season in the STAPLES Center, a $375 million multipurpose arena that includes all the modern amenities, such as skyboxes, luxury suites, and food courts. That same month, voters in Bexar County, Texas, paved the way for construction of a new $200 million home arena for the NBA World Champion San Antonio Spurs.

Surveys of professional sports franchises reveal that 77 percent of National Hockey League (NHL) franchises, 76 percent of NBA franchises, 70 percent of major league baseball franchises and 65 percent of NFL franchises, have either recently moved into new facilities or are planning or building new facilities.

A $1.6 MILLION RENOVATION CREATED THE NEW LOOK OF THE ARCHITECTURALLY DISTINCTIVE SAN DIEGO CONVENTION CENTER, AND A CURRENT RENOVATION WILL EXPAND ITS SIZE TO 2.6 MILLION SQUARE FEET.

Public assembly facilities are enjoying a boom unprecedented in the history of the industry. And that's because more and more people around the world are attending events, ranging from professional sports contests to tractor pulls, from world-class drama to fishing and travel shows, from rock concerts to high school band contests, at public assembly facilities.

TWO
CORPORATE PROFILES

PUBLIC ASSEMBLY BUILDINGS

MILLER BREWING COMPANY

SINCE 1855 A MAKER OF QUALITY BEERS ENJOYED TODAY BY MILLIONS OF BEER DRINKERS IN THE U.S.A. AND WORLD-WIDE, MILLER BREWING COMPANY CELEBRATES BASEBALL WITH MILLER PARK™, MILWAUKEE'S NEW MAJOR LEAGUE STADIUM.

Although most businesses are largely known by their products and services, some are more accurately seen in a broader community context. Miller Brewing Company is one of these and has been since its founding in Milwaukee, Wisconsin, by 19th-century German immigrant Frederick Miller.

Miller mastered the art of brewing by working in his uncle's brewery in Nancy, France, before becoming a brewmaster for Germany's royal family, the Hohenzollerns, at the Castle of Sigmaringen on the Danube. He and his wife and infant son emigrated to the United States in 1854, reportedly bringing with them $9,000 in gold—a huge sum for those days—and a year later, settled in Milwaukee, which was a growing city with a large community of German immigrants. In 1856, Miller purchased the Plank Road Brewery just west of Milwaukee and rolled out 300 barrels of sparkling lager that first year.

SUCCESS AND A CONVIVIAL SETTING

Even as he worked to make his brewery thrive, Miller began landscaping 20 acres on the hilltop overlooking the brewery and built a beer garden with a view of Lake Michigan, about three miles to the east. On weekends and holidays during the summer, Miller's Garden welcomed throngs of families, who enjoyed music and other entertainments along with hearty fare while "sipping their amber lager."

MILLER LITE BEER IS MILLER BREWING COMPANY'S NUMBER ONE BRAND.

MILLER BREWING COMPANY BREWS ITS QUALITY BEERS, SUCH AS MILLER LITE, MILLER GENUINE DRAFT, AND MILLER HIGH LIFE, IN LARGE BREW KETTLES LIKE THESE AT ITS MILWAUKEE BREWERY AND SIX OTHER BREWERIES NATIONWIDE.

Although Milwaukee's expansion swept the lovely garden into nostalgic history by 1909, the strong association of Miller Brewing Company and its quality beers with community recreation still characterizes the company.

At the end of Miller's life, in 1888, the brewery was making 80,000 barrels of beer each year; by 1954, under the leadership of Frederick Miller's grandson Frederick C. Miller, Miller Brewing Company had become the nation's ninth largest brewery. During 1969 and 1970 the company was bought by Philip Morris Companies Inc., and by 2000, Miller—the second largest brewer in the United States—was selling more than 44 million barrels of beer annually, generating operating revenues that exceed $4 billion.

In addition to its flagship brewery and corporate headquarters in Milwaukee, Miller Brewing Company operates plants in North Carolina, Georgia, Texas, Ohio, California, and the state of Washington.

Miller's direct employment of 6,600 men and women is but the core of its vital economic impact across the nation and around the world. Miller's beers are sold and distributed to retailers in the United States, Puerto Rico, and the U.S. Virgin Islands by a network of some 500 independently owned beer wholesalers. Miller brands are sold in some 100 markets abroad.

A Grand New Baseball Stadium

Beer is associated by many with celebrations and recreational activity, including sports. Few traditions seem more American than enjoying a beer at a baseball game. So it is not surprising that in 1996 Miller Brewing Company teamed up with the Milwaukee Brewers™ to purchase the naming rights for Milwaukee's grand new baseball stadium scheduled to open in April 2001: Miller Park™.

Miller's commitment to the ballpark amounts to more than $40 million. The 43,000-seat split-bowl design includes four levels, each cantilevered slightly over the one below to give fans an intimate view of the action. The stadium's unique fan-shaped retractable roof weighs 12,200 tons. Its seven panels can be left open to bring needed sunshine to the natural grass playing field and take only about 10 minutes to close, should storm clouds threaten.

RENDERED HERE, MILWAUKEE'S MILLER PARK™, ONE OF THE FINEST MAJOR LEAGUE BASEBALL™ STADIUMS, FEATURES THE ONLY FAN-SHAPED, RADIAL, RETRACTABLE ROOF IN NORTH AMERICA. THE BALLPARK, SCHEDULED TO OPEN IN APRIL 2001, MIXES A TURN-OF-THE-CENTURY BRICK EXTERIOR WITH STATE-OF-THE-ART TECHNOLOGY THROUGHOUT.

Corporate Citizenship and Responsibility

Beer has always been a part of America's celebrations. Yet with the consumption of beer comes responsibility. Miller is a leader in the brewing industry in promoting responsible drinking and is committed to fighting drunk driving and underage drinking. Miller's "Think When You Drink" national advertising campaign reminds beer drinkers about the importance of consuming beer responsibly. The company offers a variety of programs and materials, including: the *Let's Talk* parent's guide; the "Special Event Planning Kit" for special-event planners and community organizations; training for alcohol beverage retailers' servers and employees; the "Last Call" safe ride home program; a driver license booklet to help retailers and law enforcement officers verify proof of age; and college campus community programs to reduce underage drinking.

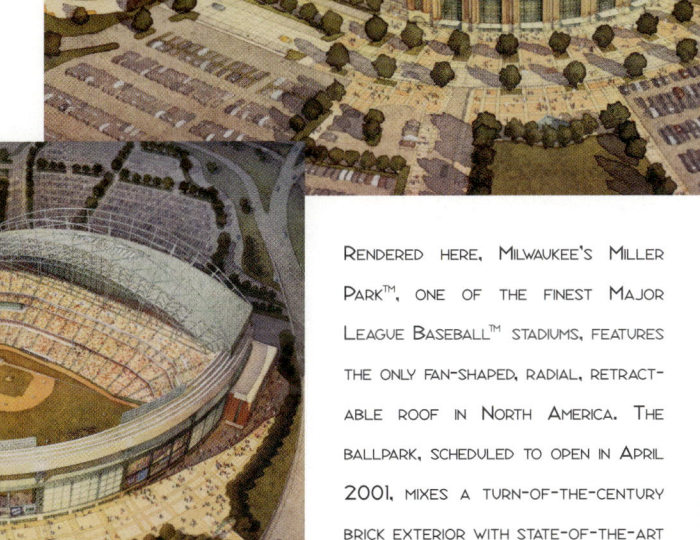

And so, when the ball is tossed onto the Miller Park infield on Opening Day 2001, the men and women of Miller Brewing Company will join their friends and neighbors in celebrating an exciting new chapter in American sport. They will also celebrate another proof of their company's unwavering commitment to the future of its home city and to the diverse communities it serves all across the nation.

LAS VEGAS CONVENTION AND VISITORS AUTHORITY

THE LAS VEGAS CONVENTION AND VISITORS AUTHORITY HAS BEEN INSTRUMENTAL IN DEVELOPING LAS VEGAS INTO ONE OF THE WORLD'S PREMIER CONVENTION AND TRADE SHOW SITES.

THE 1959 PHOTOGRAPH ABOVE SHOWS THE MAIN ENTRANCE AND ROTUNDA OF THE LAS VEGAS CONVENTION CENTER WHEN IT WAS FIRST CONSTRUCTED. AT RIGHT IS A PRESENT-DAY VIEW. © LAS VEGAS NEWS BUREAU

In 1955, the Nevada Legislature founded the Clark County Fair and Recreation Board, the precursor of the Las Vegas Convention and Visitors Authority (LVCVA), specifically to bring visitors and convention delegates to Las Vegas and Clark County.

Las Vegas had particular issues to resolve at the time of the LVCVA's creation: The cyclical nature of tourism left rooms vacant and facilities unused during midweek, throughout the hot summer months, and over the holiday season. The LVCVA targeted a new market—convention attendees—to fill rooms during these slow periods.

On April 29, 1959, the Las Vegas Convention Center officially opened with a 20,340-square-foot rotunda, 18 meeting rooms, and a 90,000-square-foot exhibit hall. In its first year of operation, the Las Vegas Convention Center hosted eight conventions, attended by 22,519 delegates.

By 1999, the Convention Center had expanded to 1.9 million square feet; citywide, Las Vegas had 5.9 million square feet of meeting and exhibit space. Las Vegas hosted more than 3,800 conventions and trade shows, attended by 3.8 million delegates. Today, a Convention Center expansion of 1.4 million square feet is under way, at a cost of $150 million. Upon completion in late 2001, the Convention Center will comprise 3.3 million square feet of space.

CONVENTION AND TRADE SHOW GROWTH

Since its inception, the LVCVA has been successful in fulfilling its mission: attracting, in steadily increasing numbers, visitors and convention delegates to the region. As Las Vegas has evolved into the "Entertainment Capital of the World," strategies used by the LVCVA to accomplish its mission have grown in scope and sophistication.

In the past decade, the number of convention delegates has more than doubled, from 1.7 million to 3.8 million annually, and the delegates' economic impact on the city has more than tripled. Nongaming spending by convention attendees reached $4.2 billion in 1999. Revenue generated by these convention delegates reaches staggering amounts,

THIS LIVELY SCENE SHOWS THE MAIN EXHIBIT HALL OF THE LAS VEGAS CONVENTION CENTER DURING COMDEX/FALL 1999. © LAS VEGAS NEWS BUREAU

CASHMAN CENTER IN LAS VEGAS PROVIDES THE FLEXIBILITY OF TWO ADJOINING, DIVISIBLE EXHIBIT HALLS TOTALING NEARLY 100,000 CONTIGUOUS SQUARE FEET, PLUS EXPANSIVE MEETING ROOMS, A BROADWAY-STYLE THEATER, AND THE 10,000-SEAT OUTDOOR STADIUM SHOWN HERE. © LAS VEGAS NEWS BUREAU

and the livelihood of the community depends on it. More than one quarter of the 1.4 million residents of Clark County work in the hotel, gaming, and convention industry.

Cashman Center

Also part of the LVCVA, Cashman Center is just minutes from downtown's casino center. Its proximity to Interstate 15 also affords easy access to the Las Vegas Strip.

With two adjoining, divisible exhibit halls providing 98,100 square feet of contiguous exhibit space, a Broadway-style theater, an outdoor stadium, and complete food and beverage facilities on site, Cashman Center is perhaps the most flexible convention and public event facility in the industry.

Additionally, Cashman Center has 16 meeting rooms, yielding another 17,500 square feet of exhibit space. Various meeting room combinations provide seating arrangements for groups ranging from 100 to 448 people. Plans to double the capacity of Cashman Center are in the works.

Overview of 1999 Conventions

Las Vegas routinely hosts more of the Tradeshow Week 200—the largest trade shows in the nation—than any other U.S. city. Las Vegas again topped Chicago as the most popular megashow site in 1999, hosting 34 of the nation's 200 largest trade shows, a 17 percent market share.

Las Vegas also rented more net square feet of exhibit space in 1999 than any other city—over 17 million square feet—maintaining a 25.1 percent market share in this category.

Some of the largest trade shows held in Las Vegas include COMDEX/Fall, the International Consumer Electronics Show, Men's Apparel Guild in California (MAGIC), National Association of Broadcasters, and NetWorld+Interop.

Convention Center Expansion

Since its construction in 1959, the Las Vegas Convention Center has expanded dramatically to accommodate the city's increasing popularity as a convention destination.

The latest expansion of the Convention Center follows a master plan set in place in 1992. In late 1998, the completion of the North Hall increased the Convention Center's total size to 1.9 million square feet. Currently under way, the South Hall expansion will take the Convention Center's total footprint to more than 3.2 million square feet. A new lobby and meeting room structure that spans Desert Inn Road, a major thoroughfare, will join the South Hall expansion to the existing facility.

When the South Hall expansion is completed, in late 2001, Las Vegas will have approximately 7.5 million square feet of convention and meeting space citywide.

World-Class Convention Destination

Las Vegas is convention friendly. No matter where delegates gather, they find the city an extremely convenient place to meet. Fine dining, resort hotels, first-rate entertainment, and of course, gaming opportunities that are second to none, have earned Las Vegas status worldwide. To accommodate its thriving national and international markets, the city offers more than 123,000 hotel rooms, about 80,000 of which are within three miles of the Las Vegas Convention Center.

SHOWN IN THIS ARCHITECTURAL RENDERING IS THE LAS VEGAS CONVENTION CENTER'S SOUTH HALL EXPANSION, WHICH IS SCHEDULED FOR COMPLETION BY DECEMBER 2001. © DOMINGO CAMBEIRO ARCHITECTS

STEPHEN C. O'CONNELL CENTER
UNIVERSITY OF FLORIDA

THE MULTIPURPOSE, STATE-OF-THE-ART STEPHEN C. O'CONNELL CENTER OFFERS ARENA SEATING FOR 12,500,

WITH ADDITIONAL ACTIVITY AREAS FOR 1,000, AND PROVIDES 51,000 SQUARE FEET OF SPACE FOR TRADE SHOWS.

THE STEPHEN C. O'CONNELL CENTER WAS UPDATED THROUGHOUT IN 1998, INCLUDING A NEW, STEEL SPACE-FRAME ROOF THAT RETAINS THE ORIGINAL DOMELIKE SHAPE.

Once an innovator, always an innovator. This is the story of the trendsetting Stephen C. O'Connell Center—an arena for athletics, recreation, and entertainment, located at the University of Florida in Gainesville.

The O'Connell Center first made history in 1980 as one of the nation's first public assembly arenas with an innovative air-supported fabric roof. The domed shape, made with translucent Teflon-coated fiberglass, was a design triumph of its time: lightweight, practical, and economical to build. Now the center again leads its industry as the nation's first arena to have an air-supported roof replaced with today's innovation—a lightweight steel roof manufactured and installed by Metro Structures. The new roof is more durable, more energy efficient, economical to maintain, and strong enough to support the elaborate rigging of today's events. The roof was replaced under the direction of structural engineers Walter P. Moore & Associates, Inc., in a record 12 weeks, a project that won the 1999 Engineering Excellence Grand Award from the Florida Institute of Consulting Engineers.

The major renovations that began in 1998 transformed the O'Connell Center into a state-of-the-art, multipurpose arena for the 21st century. In addition to the roof replacement, the center features enhanced seating and systems for sound, lighting, rigging, and special effects. The theatrical grid 78 feet above the floor is capable of supporting up to 120,000 pounds of equipment, and the new lighting system features full blackout capability, allowing afternoon events. The benefits of the renovation were immediate as proven by the sold-out Elton John concert in spring 1999—12,500 seats were filled . . . a record for the building.

The center's seating configuration offers flexibility that is rare among college campus arenas. Retractable seating on two of the three levels makes the center popular for banquets, lectures, and expositions (it offers 51,000 square feet of exhibit space). In addition to the arena, more than 1,000 people can participate simultaneously in at least nine different activities within the complex by utilizing the Olympic-size swimming pool, gymnastics studio, dance studio, martial arts studio, and practice courts, all housed within the center.

The O'Connell Center has been a crowd pleaser since its dedication in the name of the Honorable Stephen C. O'Connell, the ninth president of the University of Florida. As a leading sports and entertainment venue that attracts tens of thousands of people from Gainesville and the surrounding Orlando, Tampa, and Jacksonville areas, the Stephen C. O'Connell Center *is* the heart of entertainment in North Central Florida.

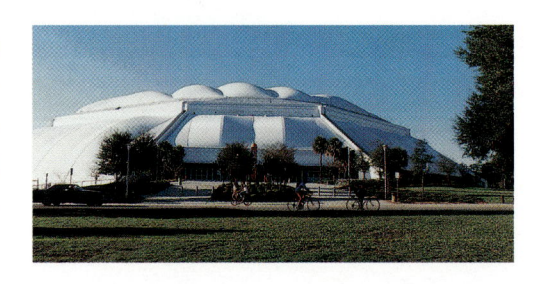

UNIVERSITY OF FLORIDA

THE O'CONNELL CENTER'S ORIGINAL AIR-SUPPORTED ROOF OF 1980 WAS A DESIGN TRIUMPH OF ITS TIME.

DALLAS CONVENTION CENTER

WITH MORE THAN 800,000 SQUARE FEET OF EXHIBIT SPACE, 105 MEETING ROOMS, TWO BALLROOMS, A THEATER, AN ARENA, AND WIRELESS INTERNET SERVICE, THE DCC CAN ACCOMMODATE CONVENTIONS OR MEETINGS OF ANY SIZE.

It is not surprising that Dallas, one of the fastest expanding metropolitan areas in the nation, boasts the largest convention complex in Texas and one of the largest in the country. What is particularly pleasing to meeting and convention organizers is that the Dallas Convention Center (DCC) is so versatile and inviting.

Located in the heart of the downtown Dallas central business district, the Dallas Convention Center is designed to accommodate any type of meeting. In fact, when the current expansion and renovations are completed, it will offer more services and amenities than ever before, making it one of the most popular convention centers in the United States.

A current major expansion, scheduled for summer 2002 completion, includes the addition of more than 200,000 square feet of contiguous prime exhibit space, creating more than 800,000 square feet of same-level, prime space. The DCC also features an additional 225,000 square feet of exhibit space on a second level below the main floor, and 105 meeting rooms. In addition, the DCC offers a 7,428-seat arena with space for 2,388 additional temporary seats and two ballrooms. The ballrooms include a 27,000-square-foot space seating up to 2,700 people theater-style and up to 1,800 for banquets, and a second ballroom space with nearly 20,000 square feet and seating up to 1,914 for meetings and approximately 1,280 for banquets. Also included in the master plan is future construction of a new ballroom and new meeting rooms.

THE DALLAS CONVENTION CENTER RENOVATION IS SCHEDULED TO BE COMPLETED IN 2002. LOCATED IN THE CENTRAL BUSINESS DISTRICT OF DOWNTOWN DALLAS, THE CONVENTION CENTER IS ONE OF THE LARGEST CONVENTION COMPLEXES IN THE UNITED STATES.

In another innovative development, the DCC made a name for itself as the first convention center in the world to feature wireless Internet service to visitors. The DCC is also known for displaying the world's largest bronze sculpture—a larger than life-size depiction of a Texas cattle drive—in its Pioneer Plaza.

What makes the Dallas Convention Center truly inviting is its attractive decor enhanced by the original artwork made available through the Public Arts Program sponsored by the City of Dallas.

The DCC's dedicated staff remains key to its success and popularity. Because of each employee's commitment to making every event a totally pleasurable experience, the DCC is recognized by trade groups, associations, and corporations from every corner of the nation as "one of the best-run convention centers in America."

WHEN ITS CURRENT EXPANSION IS COMPLETE, THE DALLAS CONVENTION CENTER WILL OFFER MORE SERVICES AND AMENITIES THAN EVER BEFORE.

CUMBERLAND COUNTY COLISEUM COMPLEX

WITH FIVE DISTINCTLY DIFFERENT VENUES, THE CUMBERLAND COUNTY COLISEUM COMPLEX HAS THE ABILITY TO HOST A MULTITUDE OF EVENTS, FROM CONCERTS TO ICE SHOW EXTRAVAGANZAS TO MEETINGS TO TRADE SHOWS.

THE 13,500-SEAT CROWN COLISEUM IS THE CENTERPIECE OF THE CUMBERLAND COUNTY COLISEUM COMPLEX, IN FAYETTEVILLE, NORTH CAROLINA.

Before the doors of the new $55 million coliseum in Fayetteville, North Carolina, ever opened, officials named it the Crown. The name was derived not only from the unique, exterior cable roofing design but also from the vision that this facility would become "the crown jewel" of the area community and surrounding market of more than one million people.

Since its inauguration in October 1997, the Crown has proved to be the dynamic centerpiece of the Cumberland County Coliseum Complex, composed of five distinctly different, but effective, venues: the 13,500-seat Crown Coliseum; an 11,250-square-foot prefunction hospitality/ballroom area, which joins the coliseum to the 60,000-square-foot Expo Center; and an adjacent 11,522-square-foot arena and 2,430-seat auditorium.

Kendall B. Wall, president and general manager of the complex, explains, "The total complex now offers a variety of multipurpose venues to host a multitude of events, from the largest concerts, ice shows, and three-ring circuses to any kind of meeting, exhibition, or trade show."

The Crown Coliseum is home to the Fayetteville Force, a leading Central Hockey League team. The Crown has hosted many world-class concerts, including Elton John's Medusa Tour, which was the largest grossing event since the coliseum opened in 1997, and the Bill Gaither Homecoming Tour, which had the largest attendance of any event. The Crown has also successfully hosted concerts by artists such as Reba McEntire, Brooks & Dunn, Patti LaBelle, Michael Bolton, and Alabama; shows such as WWF and WCW Wrestling, Ringling Brothers Circus, Disney On Ice, Champions on Ice, Stars on Ice, the Harlem Globetrotters, the Harper & Morgan Rodeo, the Royal Lipizzaner Stallions; and athletic events featuring the National Hockey League's Carolina Hurricanes and the Carolina Cobras of the Arena Football League.

The Cumberland County Coliseum Complex received the Prime Site Award from *Facilities & Event Management Magazine* in 1998 and 1999, when it was voted one of the top entertainment venues in the United States and Canada. The complex also won the Prime Site Award from *Facilities & Destinations Magazine* in 1999, when it was voted one of the top venues in the nation for meetings, conventions, and trade shows.

THE ICE FLOOR AT THE CROWN COLISEUM IS A FAVORITE OF THE CENTRAL HOCKEY LEAGUE HOME TEAM, THE FAYETTEVILLE FORCE, AND ICE SHOW EXTRAVAGANZAS SUCH AS DISNEY ON ICE, STARS ON ICE, AND CHAMPIONS ON ICE.

CROWN COLISEUM

Cumberland County Coliseum Complex
Crown Coliseum • Expo Center • Arena • Auditorium
1960 Coliseum Drive • PO Box 64549 • Fayetteville, NC 28306

SAN DIEGO CONVENTION CENTER CORPORATION

THE SAN DIEGO CONVENTION CENTER CORPORATION MANAGES, MARKETS, AND OPERATES THREE OF SAN DIEGO'S FINEST PUBLIC EVENT VENUES, ACHIEVING INTERNATIONAL RECOGNITION FOR QUALITY OF FACILITIES AND SERVICES.

THE SAN DIEGO CONVENTION CENTER (SHOWN HERE) IS WORLD-RENOWNED FOR ITS AWARD-WINNING CUSTOMER SERVICE AND BEAUTIFUL BAYSIDE LOCATION. © HAWKINS PROD.

The nonprofit San Diego Convention Center Corporation was created to manage, market, and operate three of San Diego's premier public venues—the San Diego Convention Center, the San Diego Concourse, and the San Diego Civic Theatre.

Since its opening in 1989, the Convention Center has developed an international reputation for its state-of-the-art facilities, five-star service, and world-class architecture. The San Diego Convention Center was named one of the top three convention centers in the world in both 1998 and 1999 by Europe's leading meetings industry trade publication, *Meetings & Incentive Travel* magazine.

The Convention Center was designed to host major conventions, trade shows, meetings, and special events. The Convention Center currently spans more than 1.7 million gross square feet, and a major expansion under way will boost its size to approximately 2.6 million square feet. The exhibit space will be increased to 615,701 square feet; meeting space will be expanded to 204,114 square feet; and 284,494 square feet will be added to the prefunction, lobby, and registration areas.

The Convention Center's expansion, opening in September 2001, ensures greater economic prosperity for the San Diego region and maintains the San Diego Convention Center's status as one of the most modern and technologically sophisticated convention and meeting facilities in the world.

The San Diego Concourse is a 300,000-square-foot multipurpose complex designed to host trade shows, conventions, meetings, conferences, banquets, consumer shows, and other activities. A $1.6 million renovation has created a new refined and elegant look for this facility.

The 2,975-seat San Diego Civic Theatre is the largest, most prestigious, and best-equipped performing arts theater in San Diego. The Civic Theatre is home to the San Diego Opera, the California Ballet Company, and the Nederlander/San Diego Playgoers Broadway Series.

Civic Theatre audiences enjoy a variety of performers, ranging from Luciano Pavarotti to Pearl Jam.

In addition, 1999 was the best year in the San Diego Civic Theatre's 35-year history of presenting Broadway shows, in terms of the number of productions, performances, attendance, and revenues.

Overall, the Civic Theatre was host to 189 performances and attracted 430,178 patrons.

A $1.6 MILLION RENOVATION CREATED A NEW REFINEMENT FOR THE MULTIPURPOSE SAN DIEGO CONCOURSE COMPLEX, WHICH HOSTS TRADE SHOWS, CONFERENCES, PERFORMANCES, AND SOCIAL ACTIVITIES.

THREE

Something for Everyone: Entertainment Options

On any given day or night in America, millions of people avail themselves of the entertainment options afforded by the nation's public assembly facilities.

It may be 15,000 people cheering on their beloved Trail Blazers at the charming Rose Garden in Portland, Oregon. It may be 5,000 Northlanders attending a mining equipment trade show at the Duluth, Minnesota, Convention and Civic Center. It may be a packed house at the Hollywood Bowl for pop music sensation Britney Spears or song stylist Tony Bennett. It could be a capacity crowd at Joe Louis Arena in Detroit watching the Red Wings play the Montreal Canadiens. It might be 10,000 people at the state fairgrounds in St. Paul, Minnesota, who turn out on a chilly night to watch a tractor pull. It might be 70,000 red-clad Cornhusker fans in Lincoln, Nebraska, rooting on their beloved University of Nebraska football team in its pursuit of another national championship.

It could be opera; a symphony orchestra concert; live theater; college basketball; a trade show; a convention; a boat, sports, or travel show; a computer exposition; an automobile exhibition; or any of hundreds of other forms of entertainment.

And what they all have in common is the public assembly facility, whether a stadium, arena, coliseum, auditorium, convention center, amphitheater, or any of dozens of architectural permutations of those basic models.

PAF managers know that all entertainment sporting events, acts, and performances—from baseball games to plays to operas to concerts—have at least five things in common. Each and every game or performance is essentially a presentation to a specific audience. Each fulfills a need for that audience. Each contains a central theme. Each requires staffing to ensure a safe, clean environment for the audience. And each creates an illusion for that audience.

From Tractor Pulls to Trade Shows

Public assembly facilities have been entertainment hosts for centuries. The ancient Romans used

Above, left to right: The ever-popular Harlem Globetrotters have been touring arenas across the country since the 1920s. • Michael Bolton takes center stage at a Memorial Day concert in Fayetteville, North Carolina. • Nebraska fans turn out in droves to watch the Cornhuskers meet Louisiana Tech in the 1998 Eddie Robinson football Classic at Tom Osborne Field. Opposite: Spectators hold their breath as two cyclists carry a man and woman across the high wire in this 1925 circus photo.

37

THREE

coliseum facilities for circuses, chariot races, and gladiatorial contests. Elizabethans enjoyed the plays of young William Shakespeare at the Globe Theatre outside London, and Americans in the 1890s rode streetcars to the ballpark, arena, or theater at the end of the line where they were entertained with everything from baseball and burlesque to plays and Wild West shows.

It was the turn of the 20th century, however, that marked the beginning of a mass-market entertainment phenomenon in North America that has continued—and intensified—to this day. Sports and public assembly facilities went hand in hand throughout the last century. For many families, baseball was a unifying thread that tied together generations for more than 100 years.

In the spring of 1999, an 85-year-old baseball fan accompanied his middle-aged son-in-law to see a spring training game between the Minnesota Twins and the Cincinnati Reds at the Lee County Sports Complex near Fort Myers, Florida. As they watched Johnny Bench throw out the first ball, they talked about the great Reds teams of the past, the Big Red Machine of the early 1970s, the power hitting of first baseman Ted Kluzewski in the 1950s, and the powerhouse teams of Ernie Lombardi, Bucky Walters, and Frank McCormick in 1939 and 1940.

The octogenarian had grown up during the 1920s and 1930s rooting for the Reds. Crosley Field in Cincinnati was built in 1912, two years before he was born, and he had seen many games over the years in the old concrete and steel structure in the Queen City's downtown area before it was demolished in 1969 to make way for Riverfront Stadium.

But as they sat in the stands that warm Florida afternoon, the old man took his son-in-law even further back into baseball history. He spoke of his own father's love for the then Cincinnati Redlegs. Born in the Ohio River town of Madison, Indiana, 11 years before America celebrated the turn of the new century, the old man's father attended his first Redlegs game at Redlands Stadium in 1904. The thought occurred to the two men

ABOVE: FOUNDED IN 1980, THE WORLD WRESTLING FEDERATION (WWF) HAS ATTAINED GLOBAL ENTERTAINMENT STATUS, RELYING HEAVILY ON LIVE EVENTS TO BUILD ITS FOLLOWING. RIGHT: LONG BEFORE THERE WAS WWF, THE ANCIENT ROMANS KNEW A THING OR TWO ABOUT CREATING THRILLS WITH PUBLIC EVENTS SUCH AS THIS CHARIOT RACE (CIRCA 100 A.D.).

SOMETHING FOR EVERYONE

People at the July 1999 Macworld Expo at New York's Jacob Javits Convention Center "self-register" on site. Thousands came to hear about—and get their hands on—new hardware and software, including Apple's consumer laptop, the iBook.

that they were upholding a tradition that goes back 100 years.

The younger man's son-in-law will carry on that tradition into the 21st century when they meet to cheer on the Reds at Cinergy Field, the new name given to Riverfront Stadium in 1996. And his children and grandchildren will one day sit in the stands of a new Reds ballpark, scheduled to open in 2003, and watch as records are broken and legends are made.

This family's experience with baseball is repeated in millions of families across America. Fenway Park in Boston dates back to 1912, and Wrigley Field in Chicago is still the home of the Cubs 84 years after it opened in 1916. How many families are there in Philadelphia, Pittsburgh, Detroit, and New York where grandparents tell their grandchildren about watching the

High-Tech vs. High-Touch

Radio, television, videotape, the Internet: The advent of each led to predictions that people would no longer gather in public places to be entertained. But attendance at public assembly facilities has never been better. Author and visionary John Naisbitt offers some insights into this phenomenon in his book, *High Tech/High Touch: The Co-Evolution of Technology and Culture*. In a 1998 interview, Naisbitt said, "The more technology we introduce into our society, the more people want to be with people—at movies, at rock concerts, shopping, in restaurants, at the office.... People do not go to a movie theater just to see a movie; they go to a movie to cry or laugh with 200 other people." • Likewise, people go to a stadium or ballpark to join thousands of others in cheering on their team, or to a stage play to share their laughter and applause with both the actors onstage and 500 other spectators. While technology broadens the range of entertainment options, it intensifies people's hunger for community, a hunger that public assembly facilities have been satisfying for millennia.

Entertainment Options

THREE

40

SOMETHING FOR EVERYONE

LEFT: MEMBERS OF THE CHICAGO CUBS STAND NEAR A DUGOUT IN NEWLY BUILT WRIGLEY FIELD CIRCA 1914. THE CUBS ARE PART OF AN AMERICAN BASEBALL TRADITION THAT BEGAN IN THE 19TH CENTURY. OPPOSITE: KNOWN AS "ICE MAIDENS," THESE CAST MEMBERS OF HOLIDAY ON ICE 1960 POSE AT LONDON'S EMPIRE POOL, WEMBLEY. PRODUCER MORRIS CHALFEN BROUGHT THE SHOW TO THE FOUR CORNERS OF THE WORLD.

Phillies play at Shibe Park, the Pirates play at Forbes Field, the Tigers play at Briggs Stadium, the Dodgers play at Ebbets Field, or the Giants play at the Polo Grounds?

Fathers and sons, mothers and daughters, have watched baseball, the great American game, in "fields of dreams" that have ranged from the Wrigley and Crosley Fields era to the domed stadiums of the 1960s to retro-look stadiums such as Oriole Park and Jacobs Field to the high-technology ballparks of the modern era, such as Bank One Ballpark in Phoenix and SAFECO Field in Seattle.

But it isn't just baseball they go to see. How many millions of Americans have seen a football game at Notre Dame Stadium or Lambeau Field in Green Bay or Texas Stadium in Irving? The five biggest stadiums in America—Michigan Stadium at the University of Michigan in Ann Arbor, California's Rose Bowl in Pasadena, Beaver Stadium at Pennsylvania State University in State College, Ohio Stadium at Ohio State University in Columbus, and Neyland Stadium at the University of Tennessee in Knoxville—all seat more than 80,000 spectators. On any given college football Saturday, nearly one-half million fans could be seated in those five stadiums alone. Multiply that by hundreds of smaller football stadiums nationwide, and game day means millions of fans in attendance each and every Saturday during the fall.

How many more millions have watched college basketball at the Pit in Albuquerque or Rupp Arena in Lexington, Kentucky, or for that matter, watched their favorite NBA team at the Charlotte Coliseum, the United Center in Chicago, or the Boston Garden? How many

PLAYING SOON IN AN ARENA NEAR YOU

According to their Web site, *Holiday on Ice* is "The Most Popular Show on Earth," having entertained over 300 million spectators between 1943 and 1997. Since its first performance in a Toledo hotel in 1943, *Holiday on Ice* has racked up a number of impressive statistics. It was the first American show to tour abroad when it entertained 275,000 in Mexico City in 1947. In 1959, *Holiday on Ice* was the first American show to play in the Soviet Union as part of a cultural exchange program. A photograph of Nikita Khrushchev posing with one of the show's performers was wired across the globe. When the company performed in the Nigerian village of Enugu in 1961, it was the first time their audience had ever seen ice. Today, *Holiday on Ice* spends $4.5 million to launch a new show featuring 50 performers and over 700 costumes, and has three or more shows running simultaneously in ice rinks around the world.

ENTERTAINMENT OPTIONS

millions of Canadians grew up watching the Canadiens in the Montreal Forum or the Maple Leafs at Maple Leaf Gardens in Toronto?

How many uncounted millions of Americans are there this century who have gone to their hometown stadium, gymnasium, arena, auditorium, or coliseum to watch their sons and daughters compete in high school and college sporting events? Who hasn't attended a professional or amateur sporting event in their lives?

And it isn't just sports that draws crowds. Paul Buck, a long-time–IAAM board member, recalled a 1972 Elvis Presley concert at the old Charlotte Auditorium in North Carolina, in which mail order tickets were sold out before the first

ABOVE: BAND LEADER DEBROY SOMERS AND HIS CHORUS LINE SET THE MOOD FOR A 1945 PERFORMANCE OF HAPPY AND GLORIOUS AT THE LONDON PALLADIUM. BELOW: THE BEATLES OPEN THEIR SECOND AMERICAN TOUR, IN AUGUST 1964, AT THE SAN FRANCISCO COW PALACE.

day's mail was all opened. The auditorium had to return more than 100,000 ticket requests in one week's time.

Since the 1920s, when vaudeville stars put on touring shows across the United States, Americans have been in love with musical entertainment. Whether it is a rock concert, a Big Band performance, a touring choir group, or the Three Tenors, musical shows can be expected to perform to enthusiastic audiences wherever they tour. It has not been uncommon for a popular rock group such as the Rolling Stones or the Grateful Dead to gross more than $100 million in a single season's tour of 75 or 100 cities.

As early as 1900, top-billing entertainment acts commanded $250 to $1,000 a week at the nation's theaters, an immense sum at a time when mens' and boys' suits retailed for $6.85, and a pair of handmade women's leather shoes could be purchased for as little as $2.50 a pair.

In the first half of the 20th century, Americans flocked to arenas, auditoriums, and other public assembly facilities to watch vaudeville, burlesque, ice shows, and circuses. By the 1920s, the nation's theaters had been converted to show talking motion pictures, one of the cheapest forms of entertainment for Americans, who were weighed down by the economic woes of the Great Depression.

SOMETHING FOR EVERYONE

Movies continued to be popular through the war years and after, creating spin-off opportunities for live entertainment. In the big cities, nightclubs and auditoriums showcased the talents of Broadway and Hollywood stars. The Big Band era hit full swing during the war years, and Hollywood and Big Band stars ensured themselves huge new national audiences with their United Service Organizations (USO) tours of military facilities in the United States and overseas. On the home front, war workers were flush with cash for the first time in more than a decade. Since consumer durables, such as automobiles and home appliances, were unavailable at any price because of wartime restrictions, people spent money on entertainment. During and after the war, radio did its part to nurture audiences of live music, such as jazz and blues, and a new postwar medium—television—popularized wrestling and other attractions. (Television continues to be a major promoter of sports and other live entertainment today.)

Some forms of entertainment began to reach a national audience for the first time during the 1940s and 1950s. Country music—then referred to as "hillbilly music"—came into its own during this period. WLS radio in Chicago pioneered barn dance events in theaters across the Midwest; one such show grossed $9,000 in one day in Milwaukee, at a time when most theater owners thought it a huge success when their facility grossed $20,000 a week.

The 1950s and 1960s put a whole new twist on the concept of touring musical entertainment. Rock 'n' roll began a conquest of the American entertainment scene that has not largely abated since. The phenomenon characterized by Elvis Presley, the Beatles, the Rolling Stones, and the Beach Boys reached its zenith in an upstate New York cow pasture in 1969. Woodstock became an icon for an entire generation of Americans. By the 1970s, it wasn't uncommon for rock artists such as the Grateful Dead, Led Zeppelin, or Fleetwood Mac to gross $1 million or more for a single performance.

It isn't just touring musical entertainment that appeals to the mass market. The nearly 1,000 symphony orchestras in North America have been delighting fans of classical music for more than a

ABOVE: COUNTRY MUSIC STARS REBA MCENTIRE AND BROOKS & DUNN PLAY THE INAUGURAL CONCERT AT NORTH CAROLINA'S 13,500-SEAT CROWN COLISEUM IN FAYETTEVILLE IN 1997. LEFT: AMERICAN SOLDIERS IN FRANCE IN 1944 ENJOY THE FIRST USO CAMP SHOW. MANY GIS RETURNED FROM WORLD WAR II ANXIOUS TO SEE THEIR FAVORITE ENTERTAINERS PERFORM ON STAGE AT HOME.

ENTERTAINMENT OPTIONS

THREE

century. Choral groups, barbershop quartets, high school and college marching bands, string quartets, and the like perform in front of millions of people in their home communities every year.

Live theater is another constant in 20th-century American entertainment, whether it is the homegrown Missouri pageant satirized in the movie *Waiting for Guffman*; an off–off Broadway presentation of the latest David Mamet play; a new take on a Shakespearean comedy by the repertory company at upstate New York's Syracuse Stage; or a touring Broadway musical on stage in Fargo, North Dakota.

The Creative Process

In the early days of the 20th century, arenas and auditoriums in most major cities existed on a steady diet of circuses, rodeos, and touring ice shows. Those entertainment options are still with us today, but the savvy public assembly facilities manager supplements them with other shows. Every night, somewhere in America, thousands of people are in attendance at tractor pulls, indoor soccer games, wrestling matches, home shows, antiques exhibitions, and flower and garden shows.

The Las Vegas Convention Center (LVCC), which is currently undergoing a 1.4 million-square-foot expansion, already boasts 1.9 million square feet of space. Below: The center hosts the 1999 Comdex/Fall computer convention, with 2,000 exhibits and 200,000 attendees. Opposite: LVCC is the site of the annual World Gaming Congress & Expo, which brings together gaming, hospitality, and entertainment executives.

44

Something for Everyone

Due to the high cost of touring entertainment in the 1980s and 1990s, many established acts have consolidated their tours to play only in major markets and particular venues. This, coupled with increased competition between public assembly facilities, has made it necessary for PAF managers to be more creative and to consider promoting or copromoting their own events. Often the result is local and civic entertainment events aimed at a narrower slice of the consumer marketplace. Public assembly facility managers call the phenomenon "going local," and events such as rock 'n' roll revivals, video sports telecasts, specialty and ethnic food festivals, symphony "pops" concerts with celebrity guest artists, and corporate product launches often mean the difference between operating in the red and showing a profit.

With many touring acts requesting a guarantee exceeding six figures, PAF managers in smaller markets found other ways to make money in the 1990s, including weddings, corporate sponsorships, copromotions, and even full promotions by the host facility. And it is an axiom of the business that an act that plays to a full house in Biloxi, Mississippi, might not play at all well in Billings, Montana.

Americans are joiners. They belong to literally thousands of trade and professional associations, and many of those associations host national, regional, and state conventions, conferences, and seminars. There are more than 55.2 million square feet of exhibit space in the United States, and a major exhibit hall, conference center, or convention center is booked as many as 300 calendar days a year. California leads the nation in exhibit space (6.3 million square feet), followed by Texas (4.9 million square feet), Florida (4.2 million square feet), Illinois (3.8 million square feet), and Nevada (3.7 million square feet).

Conventions and trade shows are both business and entertainment. PAF managers call them "industrial theater" and point out that the goal of any good convention center manager is to create the same illusion for delegates and attendees as the manager of any stadium, auditorium, or performing arts center creates for his or her audiences.

The industrial theater aspect of conventions and trade shows is more akin to the medieval fair than it is to a James Brown concert or a San Antonio Spurs–Chicago Bulls NBA game. Delegates have to be housed, fed, and transported over a typical period of three days. That's why Las Vegas boasts of having more than 90,000 hotel rooms to serve the millions of convention and trade show attendees who pass through the city annually, and every convention center manager in America wants to have input with—or membership on—the local airport authority.

But the entertainment component of conventions and trade shows is also important, and many trade shows have at least one or two entertainment acts booked to divert the attention of weary conference-goers as they wander up and down the aisles. It is no accident that topflight touring groups such as the Dixie Chicks kept body and soul together playing trade shows on their road to the top.

Entertainment is a unifying force. From the beginning of history, people have been captivated, enthralled, and moved by the entertainment options available to them. Whether it be sports, live theater, touring musical shows, or just an evening at the movies, entertainment has enriched the lives of virtually everyone in every era.

ENTERTAINMENT OPTIONS

THREE
CORPORATE PROFILES

47

ENTERTAINMENT OPTIONS

WORLD WRESTLING FEDERATION ENTERTAINMENT, INC.

ONE OF THE MOST SUCCESSFUL, FASTEST GROWING BUSINESSES IN ENTERTAINMENT, WORLD WRESTLING FEDERATION ENTERTAINMENT, INC., HAS BUILT ITS PRODUCT AROUND THE LIVE EVENTS THAT MAKE UP ITS TELEVISION PROGRAMMING.

Through a pattern of steady growth over the past two decades, World Wrestling Entertainment, Inc. (WWFE), has established itself as a premier worldwide producer of live events, selling out arenas from Arrowhead Pond of Anaheim to New York City's Madison Square Garden to London's Earls Court and points in between. Owned and run by the McMahon family, with longtime employee Ed Cohen as senior vice president of Event Booking & Live Events, the company promotes approximately 200 events per year. A large number of these events are televised, on such programs as *Raw Is War*, the weekly series with the highest rating (Nielsen) on cable, broadcast on The Nashville Network (TNN), and *SmackDown!*, the top-rated series on United Paramount Network (UPN). One live event per month is aired on cable pay-per-view (PPV), a medium pioneered by WWFE over the past 15 years.

The key to the success of WWFE live events is the proven drawing power of the company's product brand, the World Wrestling Federation. WWFE has crafted a unique genre all its own, known as "sports-entertainment." A term coined by WWFE chairman Vincent K. McMahon, "sports-entertainment" refers to the genre's action/adventure, soap opera story lines, and comic sensibility—an innovative blend that makes up the World Wrestling Federation product. It is a proven fact that fans worldwide are attracted to WWFE live events through brand-name recognition. Events have been known to sell out in a matter of minutes, before any card information has even been announced, which can be attributed to the drawing power of the World Wrestling Federation brand.

VINCENT K. MCMAHON IS THE CHAIRMAN OF WORLD WRESTLING FEDERATION ENTERTAINMENT, INC.

FROM CHARITY TO PPV

WWFE live events have come a long way since the company's humble beginnings in 1980. Aside from the McMahons themselves, no one is in as unique a position to judge that as Ed Cohen, who has been with the company for the past 18 years.

ED COHEN IS SENIOR VICE PRESIDENT OF EVENT BOOKING & LIVE EVENTS.

"It is amazing," Cohen says. "When I started, we were booking nonprofit events in high school gymnasiums during the week. On weekends, we scheduled major arenas within our 'territory,' which included facilities from Maine to Maryland. I can't think of another live event vehicle that has demonstrated the tremendous growth that the World Wrestling Federation has experienced in such a relatively short time."

Running what was then known as Titan Sports, Vince and his wife, Linda, purchased Capitol Wrestling Corporation from Vince's father, Vincent J. McMahon, in 1982, bringing the World Wrestling Federation brand under the Titan Sports umbrella. With Cohen brought on board the same year, the McMahons began a campaign to transform a regional professional wrestling business into what is now a worldwide enterprise.

The moment when the company truly emerged as a force to be reckoned with in the live event industry occurred on March 31, 1985, when the first *WrestleMania* was held at Madison Square Garden. Not only was the primary venue sold out, but also arenas and other locations throughout the United States were filled with capacity crowds, which had come to view the event on the first-ever nationwide closed-circuit broadcast for this genre. *WrestleMania* was a rousing success, proving the viability of live events as a catalyst for revenues stretching beyond the attendance gate.

Capitalizing on the momentum of *WrestleMania*, Titan Sports broke ground in the newly emerging PPV market with the broadcast of *The Wrestling Classic* on November 7, 1985, from the Rosemont Horizon (now Allstate Arena) in suburban Chicago. On April 7, 1986, in an effort to top the previous year's outing, *WrestleMania 2* was presented in three different venues: New York's Nassau Coliseum, Chicago's Rosemont Horizon,

THE ROCK HITS THE "ROCK BOTTOM" ON TRIPLE H.

LINDA E. MCMAHON IS THE CEO OF WORLD WRESTLING FEDERATION ENTERTAINMENT, INC. © WORLD WRESTLING FEDERATION ENTERTAINMENT, INC./RICH FREEDA

and the Los Angeles Sports Arena, with a simultaneous broadcast on PPV. This was the first time any event emanated from three different cities, an achievement that has yet to be duplicated. But what is perhaps one of the company's greatest successes in live event promotion came one year later, on March 29, 1987, with *WrestleMania III* at Detroit's Pontiac Silverdome, witnessed by a sellout crowd of 93,173—an indoor attendance record for sports and entertainment events, which still stands.

Recent years have seen such triumphs as *SummerSlam '94*—which had the distinction of being the first event of any kind held at Chicago's United Center—as well as an unprecedented run of consecutive sellouts at Madison Square Garden from 1998 through 2000. In September 2000, for the first time ever, WWFE held televised events on two consecutive nights in a single major venue, at the America West Arena in Phoenix. *WrestleMania XVII*, scheduled to take place April 1, 2001, at Houston's Astrodomain Complex (formerly the Astrodome), is expected to produce the largest gross for a live event in the history of World Wrestling Federation Entertainment, Inc.

GROWING BY LEAPS AND BOUNDS

In the past several years, WWFE has entered a period of dynamic growth unprecedented in the company's history. From 1997 to 1999, net revenues increased more than 200 percent, and revenues doubled from the first fiscal quarter of 1999 to that of 2000. This kind of tremendous success is largely due to the overwhelming popularity

WORLD WRESTLING FEDERATION ENTERTAINMENT, INC. (CONTINUED)

of WWFE's live events, and the high mainstream profile attained by the company has kept the crowds coming.

"I believe that the sustained expansion of our live event business is a testament to the way in which we have managed to keep our product fresh and appealing to our fans," comments Vince McMahon.

"And it is impossible to talk about the success of our company without mentioning Ed Cohen, who has played an invaluable part in getting us to where we are today," he says.

The figures speak for themselves. Total annual attendance nearly tripled from 1996 to mid-2000. WWFE's live events are produced in approximately 100 cities in North America, as well as several prominent international locations. Revenue from ticket sales is enhanced by the on-site sale of WWFE's highly popular branded merchandise. At the company's *WrestleMania* event held at Anaheim's Arrowhead Pond, World Wrestling Federation merchandise sales generated an average of $19 per patron, a new record in the sports-entertainment business. More than 800,000 people viewed the PPV broadcast of the event, making it the most lucrative non-boxing event in PPV history.

In recent years, the question has not been *whether* tickets for a WWFE live event will sell out, but rather, how quickly. The *Judgment Day* PPV event held at Louisville's Freedom Hall on May 21, 2000, sold out in 70 minutes, making it the third-fastest sellout in the venue's 44-year history. The December 2000 international PPV event in Sheffield, England, sold out in less than an hour and a half. When tickets went on sale for *King of the Ring*, which took place at Boston's FleetCenter on Sunday, June 25, 2000, the event sold out in 4½ minutes—a WWFE record!

TRIPLE H AND "HIS WIFE," STEPHANIE MCMAHON-HELMSLEY, SHARE ONE OF LIVE WRESTLING'S HEATED MOMENTS.

SHANE MCMAHON IS PRESIDENT OF NEW MEDIA FOR WORLD WRESTLING FEDERATION ENTERTAINMENT, INC.

THE MAN BEHIND WWFE MAGIC

Ed Cohen, WWFE's senior vice president of Event Booking & Live Events, is a familiar face in the arena industry. Cohen has seen his role and responsibilities grow dramatically along with the company since he began his career in 1982. Today, he oversees the routing and marketing of approximately 200 live events scheduled throughout the world each year. Over the course of his career, Cohen has scheduled over 15,000 events, more than anyone else in the industry. In 1990, Cohen was the guest instructor at the IAAM Foundation's Public Assembly Facility Management School at Oglebay Park in Wheeling, West Virginia. In 1999, he was appointed a trustee of the IAAM Foundation.

What is in the future for WWFE? "I'd like us to hold the first event on the moon," says Cohen. Don't put it past the World Wrestling Federation.

World Wrestling Federation®

51

THE DREAM MAKERS: ARCHITECTS AND PLANNERS

To paraphrase novelist William P. Kinsella, build it and they will come. But first, you've got to design it and build it. • Public assembly facilities don't just spring from the ground, as if by magic. They are typically the result of years of planning and design by a team of architects, developers, construction companies, and subcontractors. Without the expertise of the architects and planners, and the builders who transform blueprints and computerized drawings into reality, there would be no stadiums, theaters, convention centers, or the dozens of other public assembly facilities where people gather for entertainment, sports, and work.

A Millennial Approach to Design

Public assembly facilities have design requirements that most other public and private buildings don't have to incorporate. First, they require multiple entrances that will handle the ingress and egress of thousands of people within a relatively short period of time. They demand heating, ventilating, and air-conditioning systems that can handle everything from making ice for a professional ice show to creating the heat and humidity for a flower and garden show. Public assembly facilities must contain comfortable, interchangeable seating, and the seating must be situated so that every seat in the house has an unobstructed line of sight.

Architects and planners have been designing and building public assembly facilities for millennia, and some of those designs are still with us today. The ancient Greeks gave us the concept of a stadium, a U-shaped facility utilized for footraces, and the hippodrome, essentially a racetrack built into the side of a hill to provide tiered seating for spectators.

The Romans took the concept one step further with the design and construction of the Colosseum, a huge elliptical amphitheater with seating for nearly 50,000 citizens in three tiers built on stone and concrete arches and pillars. The Roman amphitheaters and arenas were used primarily for sporting events and gladiatorial contests.

Above: Architects and planners millennia ago designed public assembly facilities with such motifs as this bas relief chariot race. Opposite: Danish architect Jørn Utzon won a 1950s competition to design the Sydney Opera House. Elements such as the roof "sails" turned out to be major engineering hurdles. Finally completed with modifications in 1973, the building has become not only a Sydney landmark, but a world symbol for Australia.

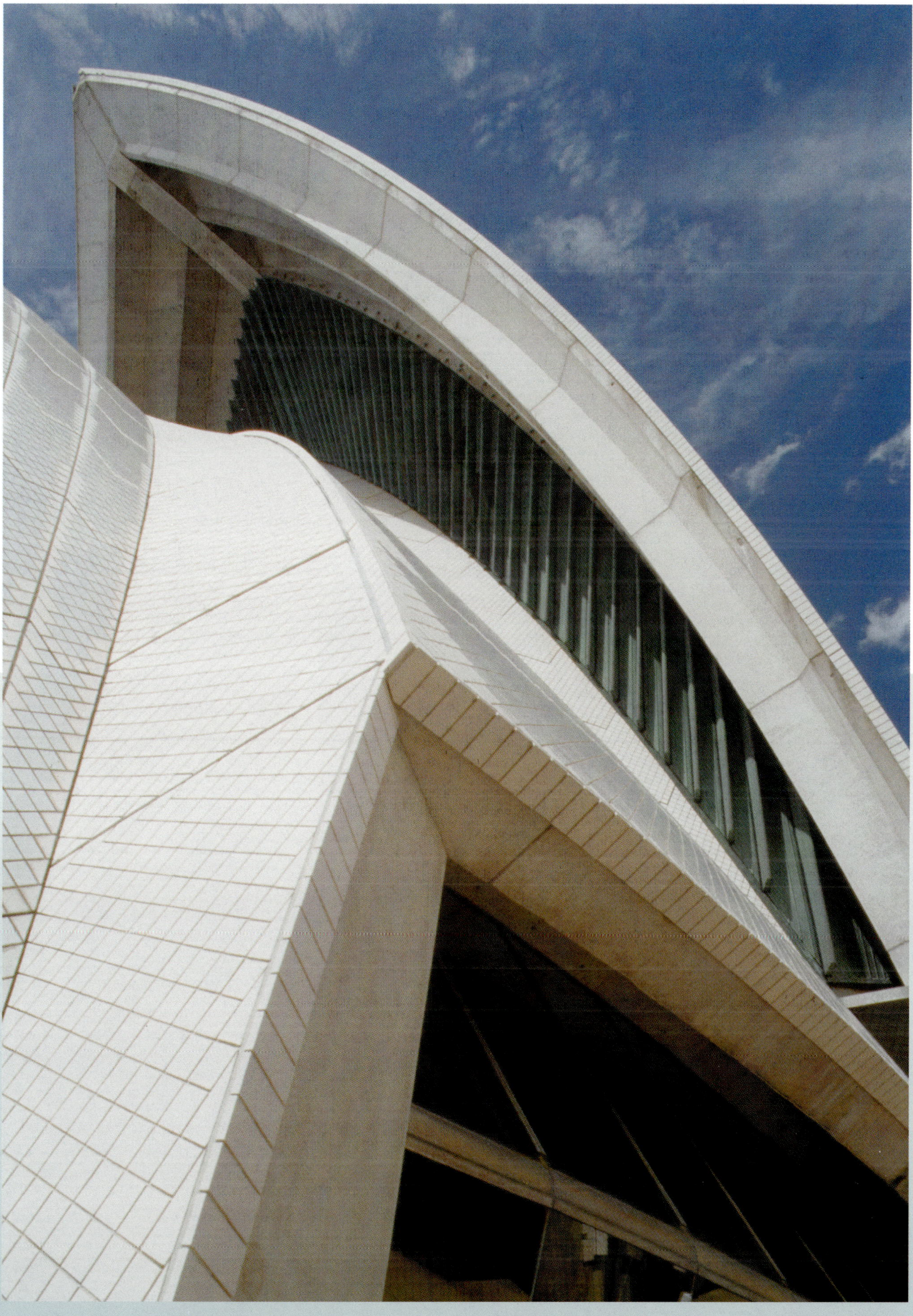

FOUR

The industrial revolution of the 18th and 19th centuries brought with it increased demand for spectator sports and entertainment events, and with the revival of the Olympic Games in the 1890s, the stadium was born anew. The modern stadium is exemplified in America by California architect John Parkinson's 1920s design for the Los Angeles Memorial Coliseum.

Nor are stadiums the only public assembly facilities with their roots deep in history. The patron of today's modern repertory theater or concert hall would likely recognize the seating arrangements, stage layout, acoustics, and orchestra pit of the Globe Theatre in London, which hosted so many of William Shakespeare's plays in the 16th century.

The tremendous popularity of spectator sports such as baseball, football, and basketball, along with the prevalence of touring entertainment in 20th-century America—from vaudeville to rock concerts—led to a virtual explosion in construction of public assembly facilities. Prosperity in the years after World War II fueled a surge in the building of stadiums, arenas, auditoriums, amphitheaters, concert halls, convention centers, and civic centers that has not abated to this day.

Facilities managers are now demanding larger, more flexible facilities, along with increased meeting and high-end ballroom space. Integrated interior design of larger lobby, prefunction, and meeting areas is a must, while satellite suburbs and cities—particularly those located near outlying airports—are designing and building smaller facilities to handle spillover from major metropolitan area centers.

Many of the public assembly facilities built today cost hundreds of millions of dollars. And a surprising number use architectural techniques that have been known for millennia.

When the city of Chicago's Metropolitan Pier and Exposition Authority (MPEA) decided to utilize the design-build approach for construction of the South Hall expansion project at McCormick Place in the early 1990s, it was adopting a construction model that is thousands of years old. Design-build involves wedding the skills of architects and contractors in a joint venture to do a turnkey construction job.

Chicago's MPEA began investigating design-build for the South Hall expansion project shortly after the North Hall Expansion project was completed in 1987. North Hall, a 500,000-square-foot facility, was originally estimated to cost just over $200 million to build; final costs were 50 percent higher.

Estimates for the South Hall expansion, including demolishing

ABOVE: THE MILWAUKEE AUDITORIUM'S BRUCE HALL OFFERS A RICH SETTING FOR THEATRICAL PRODUCTIONS AND CONCERTS. RIGHT: QUEEN ELIZABETH I (SEATED IN THE BOX UPPER LEFT) ENJOYS WILLIAM SHAKESPEARE'S THE MERRY WIVES OF WINDSOR AT THE GLOBE THEATRE IN LONDON CIRCA 1560. THE GLOBE HAS BEEN A MODEL FOR MANY MODERN PLAYHOUSES.

THE DREAM MAKERS

the 27-story McCormick Place hotel and tying together some 2.2 million square feet of exhibit space and support space, came in at between $650 and $700 million; a 50 percent cost overrun would put the project into the billion-dollar class.

The solution was to farm the project out to a design-build team that called itself Mc3D: an eight-company consortium that would be responsible for the design and construction of the project. MPEA financed the project through the sale of more than $950 million in bonds, which would be paid for through a one-dollar ground transportation tax at both of Chicago's airports, a one percent tax on prepared food and beverages in the city's central business district, a six percent tax on short-term auto leasing in Cook County,

SHOWN HERE UNDER CONSTRUCTION, THE VERSATILE 2000 OLYMPIC STADIUM, IN SYDNEY, AUSTRALIA, HAS A HYPERBOLIC PARABOLOID ROOF AND THE ABILITY TO CONVERT FROM SEATING 115,000 OLYMPIC SPECTATORS TO 60,000–80,000 FANS AT REGULAR SPORTING EVENTS.

DESIGN-BUILD THROUGH THE AGES

Design-build is a team approach to architecture and construction with a long history. There is evidence to suggest that the pharaohs used design-build teams to construct the pyramids in Egypt's Valley of the Kings, and the medieval guilds that built the great cathedrals of France and Germany were often brought together in design-build teams to construct the great monuments of European religious faiths. • The design-build concept fell out of favor beginning in the mid-19th century as the role of the architect diverged from that of the contractor. Design-build re-emerged in the United States in the late 1920s and early 1930s. Henry J. Kaiser put together the Six Companies consortium to build Hoover Dam on the Colorado River, and design-build teams were commonly used in the federal government's mammoth dam-building program on the Tennessee, Missouri, and Columbia Rivers from the 1930s to the 1950s. • Design-build became increasingly popular in the late 20th century as a method by which property owners could best control the costs as well as the quality of large construction projects.

ARCHITECTS AND PLANNERS

FOUR

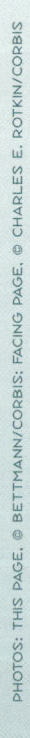

56

The Dream Makers

LEFT: THE HOUSTON ASTRODOME, THE ORIGINAL DOMED STADIUM, OPENED IN 1965. A SPATE OF ROOFED STADIUMS WOULD FOLLOW. OPPOSITE: ON APRIL 19, 1923, YANKEE STADIUM OPENS TO THE PUBLIC. IN RECENT YEARS, CITY OFFICIALS HAVE PROPOSED BUILDING A NEW $1 BILLION STADIUM ON MANHATTAN'S WEST SIDE OR EXPANDING THE EXISTING BRONX SITE TO CREATE A "YANKEE VILLAGE."

and a 2.5 percent tax on hotel rooms in Chicago.

Mc3D took the contract for a guaranteed price of $670 million. Work on the project began in 1993. Foundation work was 50 percent completed in 1994, and structural steel work began in January 1994. The South Hall itself was enclosed in December 1995. Work was completed in late 1996.

Six of the eight Mc3D partners joined together as McCormick Place Contractors, Inc., (McPC) to handle all of the construction work on the South Hall/Grand Concourse project.

Chicago's McCormick Place expansion typified the trend in convention center construction in the 1990s. To help build the $100 million Texas International Raceway north of Fort Worth from 1995 to 1997, six Texas companies teamed up in a design-build project: Terra-Mar, Inc., of Fort Worth; T.J. Lambrecht Construction of Hurst; Huitt-Zollars, Inc., of Dallas; the Sadler Group of Fort Worth; Robert T. Williams & Associates of Charlotte; and Sunmount Inc., of Justin. The Clark Construction Group of Bethesda, Maryland, came into the Mc3D project with design-build experience from the Oriole Park at Camden Yards project in Baltimore and went on to team again with Mc3D partners Thompson Ventulett Stainback & Associates (TVS) of Atlanta to design and build Milwaukee's new downtown convention center.

For the Milwaukee project, Clark Construction and TVS were joined by other designers and engineers to form Cream City Associates. Cream City won their bid to design and build Milwaukee's convention center by printing artist's renderings of the new building on postcards and passing them out to the city's selection committee.

From start to finish, the design-build team worked hard to interface with the owner and unions to resolve problems. For example, the original design called for the building to be made of steel. But cost concerns led the design-build team to switch to structural concrete for much of the construction, a change that required union cooperation.

Milwaukee's 667,000-square-foot, $167 million Midwest Express Center opened to the public in July 1998 to rave reviews, even before its completion in December 1999. The center has been praised for integrating artfully with Milwaukee's traditional architecture while providing modern, richly appointed spaces.

THE EVOLUTION OF DESIGN

Tastes change. Styles change. Games change. And architects and designers are keenly aware that what might have served the needs of fans of spectator sports early in the 20th century might well be outmoded for 21st-century fans.

Modern adaptations include such advances as air-conditioning, cantilever construction to increase usable floor space and improve sight lines, telescopic seating systems to modify seating for different types of events, and sophisticated sound and lighting systems for arenas and stadiums.

ARCHITECTS AND PLANNERS

FOUR

Design improvements made to baseball stadiums in the past 90 years illustrate this evolution.

In the early years of the 20th century, designers and architects built some of baseball's most memorable "fields of dreams". Some legendary fields still have their legions of fans. These include Boston's Fenway Park (built in 1912), Chicago's Wrigley Field (1914), and New York's Yankee Stadium (1923). But many of the early-20th-century stadiums were cramped, lines of sight were often obstructed by exposed girders, and bathrooms and concession stands were often woefully inadequate. Later generations of planners and architects would have the technology and experience to avoid these design problems.

Some of the grand old ballparks gave decades of service to devoted fans before being replaced by modern facilities. When Tiger Stadium closed in Detroit in September 1999, the venerable old ballpark had been hosting Motor City fans for 88 years.

The Great Depression and World War II essentially precluded the construction of new baseball stadiums in America for nearly a quarter-century. After the war, new technologies enabled baseball to be played indoors. And a postwar demographic shift of population to the hot Southeast and Southwest dictated that air-conditioning would become a fact of life for the public assembly facility business, even for games that were traditionally played outdoors.

In 1965, the Houston Astrodome opened, becoming the first air-conditioned, domed stadium in the world. Judge Roy Hofheinz, then president of the city's major league baseball team, the Astros, wanted a venue that would allow spectators to watch baseball indoors, protected from the city's hot, humid, and rainy climate.

Two innovative Houston architectural firms, Lloyd and Morgan, and Wilson, Morris, Crain and Anderson, had to deal with a host of soil, temperature, and sunlight issues never faced before by stadium designers. They had planned for the Astrodome to have real grass, grown under natural light shining through semitransparent roof panels. But the outfielders had trouble seeing balls against the glare of the skylights, and once the skylights were painted, the grass wouldn't grow. So the Astrodome was fitted with synthetic turf, another innovation that changed the way baseball and football were played in America in the late 20th century.

The success of the Astrodome spawned a slew of covered stadiums in the next 20 years, from Seattle to Minneapolis. These included the technologically sophisticated inflatable roofing used in stadiums such as the Hubert H. Humphrey Metrodome in Minneapolis, Minnesota, and BC Place Stadium in Vancouver, British Columbia.

CHICAGO'S MCCORMICK PLACE FEATURES A 50,000-SQUARE-FOOT GLASS-ENCLOSED PROMENADE CALLED THE GRAND CONCOURSE (STRUCTURE ON LEFT), WHICH OFFERS A MYRIAD OF SHOPS AND SERVICES. ON THE RIGHT IS THE WEST ENTRANCE TO THE NEW SOUTH BUILDING.

But baseball fans didn't always like the sterile atmosphere of the domes, arguing that baseball should be played outdoors on real grass. Fans told the designers and builders that they enjoyed the intimacy of earlier parks, such as Brooklyn's Ebbets Field, and architects responded in the 1990s with a new generation of baseball parks. Oriole Park at Camden Yards in Baltimore ushered in the new trend in 1992, utilizing the design of Hellmuth, Obata & Kassabaum (HOK) of

THE DREAM MAKERS

Kansas City, Missouri. Jacobs Field in Cleveland was designed as a modernistic antithesis to Oriole Park in 1994, while the Ballpark in Arlington, Texas, which also opened in 1994, more closely followed the HOK model for Oriole Park, paying homage to the original Comiskey Park in Chicago and Fenway Park in Boston.

In the late 1990s, the revival look of baseball parks so popular in the early and mid-decade gave way to a variation: high-technology ballparks with retractable roofs and amenities ranging from swimming pools to hardwired luxury suites to video game arcades for the kids. Bank One Ballpark in Phoenix and SAFECO Field in Seattle typified the new trend.

Kansas City–based HNTB has been at the forefront of design of minor league baseball parks as minor league baseball has enjoyed its greatest growth ever. The firm has designed and built new parks in Sevier County, Tennessee; Dayton, Ohio; Sacramento, California; Louisville, Kentucky; and Suffolk County, New York—all of which opened during 2000—and is in the process of designing and building minor league parks in Lakewood, New Jersey; Peoria, Illinois; Stockton, California; and Toledo, Ohio. HNTB is currently designing and building the new Mile High Stadium in Denver, as well as overseeing major renovation projects at California's Oakland–Alameda County Coliseum and the Los Angeles Memorial Coliseum.

Another major national architectural and engineering company is Ellerbe Becket. Based in Minneapolis, Ellerbe Becket is the third largest architecture and engineering firm in the United States. Ellerbe Becket was responsible for the much-publicized implosion of the Seattle Kingdome in early 2000 and is currently building a 67,000-seat stadium to replace the Seattle landmark. Ellerbe Becket architects and engineers designed and built the retractable-roofed Bank One Ballpark in Phoenix and Turner Field in Atlanta. The company completed the historic renovation of the Notre Dame Football Stadium in South Bend, Indiana, and Madison Square Garden in New York City. Ellerbe Becket also assisted in the design of Japan's new state-of-the-art Saitama Super Arena outside Tokyo, which can accommodate virtually any type of event from an intimate concert to a football game.

Looking at recent projects undertaken by these and other prominent architects and planners, it is clear that arenas hosting basketball and hockey have evolved alongside ballparks and stadiums in their complex of activities and events. And much of what is pioneered in sports facility design and construction soon shows up in other public assembly facilities—and vice versa.

Public assembly facilities compete with one another for teams and entertainment bookings, and must be constantly on the lookout for ways to distinguish themselves from other venues. This competition is at the heart of a 1997 article by David Greusel of HOK in which he heralded a convergence of sports and entertainment facilities that calls for sports venues to have themes, much like modern-day amusement parks such as Walt Disney World and Dollywood. As public assembly facilities face the added challenge of creating the complete spectator experience, it is the planners, architects, engineers, designers, and builders who will help them meet that challenge with the same creativity and resourcefulness they have employed through a century of change.

Olympic Proportions

Designing the Sydney 2000 Olympic Stadium involved many challenges. Stadium specifications called for "ecologically sustainable development," as well as the capacity to seat crowds of over 100,000 for the two-week games and the flexibility to scale down for later events so that spectators would still feel close to the action. The Australian Stadium 2000 Consortium, headed by Multiplex Construction and Hambros Australia, drew together a design team to meet these challenges. The team ultimately chose the concept of Bligh Lobb Sports Architecture, a joint venture of London-based Lobb Partnership and a major Australian architecture firm, Bligh Voller. Bligh Lobb's design had safety and intimacy as its paramount goals, and used a computer system called Microstation 95 for rapid design and modification. The completed stadium is beautiful, functional, and maintainable far beyond the Olympic Games.

PROCESSES AND TOOLS

The process of designing and building a new public assembly facility—whether for a performing arts center, a convention center, or a new sports stadium—is complex and time-consuming. Selection of a competent architectural firm is a crucial first step in the process.

The architect provides the sponsoring organization with a wide variety of services, including the initial schematic design; development of the design concept; preparation of the construction documents, including drawings and specifications; assistance in the request-for-proposal process; and administration and oversight of the contractor agreements.

One of the first decisions that the governing authority has to make is whether to secure the services of a local architect or a national firm with the reputation for building innovative public assembly facilities. Increasingly, sponsors are bridging the gap by selecting a national firm that partners with a local firm, creating a blend of local and national expertise.

The selection of an engineering consultant is also a critical part of the process. Engineering consultants can help the architect with the tremendously complex requirements of designing and building public assembly facilities, including all-important building and life safety codes compliance.

The engineering consultant is also often a specialty consultant. Building diagnostics, a science that emerged during the 1990s, is a key component in the design and construction of most new public assembly facilities. Hundreds of thousands of cubic feet of air move around and through the typical public assembly facility, and engineers take pains to ensure that heating, ventilation, and air-conditioning systems are designed to eliminate moisture and expedite the flow of fresh air.

Then there's the matter of dividing rooms in convention centers and civic centers with acoustical panels. Several manufacturing firms specialize in providing the space divider panels that allow multipurpose facilities to make the optimum use of their space.

Dusk falls over the Midwest Express Center in downtown Milwaukee. The new convention facility offers advanced information technology service and voice/data communications in its 188,695 square feet of exhibit space and 28 meeting rooms.

Thanks to the computer, architects, planners, and designers have new tools to use in designing public assembly facilities that their predecessors could only have dreamed of using. Perhaps the biggest breakthrough in the past quarter-century was the emergence of computer-aided design (CAD) software. Now, with the click of a mouse, an architect can create drawings, plans, and schematic renderings of objects. An architect working with a design team for a convention or civic center can change specifications for a ballroom or meeting room almost instantaneously.

Similarly, computers have revolutionized the entire design and building process. Facilities managers are now able to use an off-the-shelf word processing program to create standard contracts and requests for proposal, as well as to keep track of the complex process of booking and billing acts. The construction manager can create and update a detailed timeline that will keep the project on deadline and under budget.

Architects and designers are plugging in sophisticated new technology updates when they create schematics for new convention centers and stadiums. St. Louis's recently opened America's Center boasts fiber-optic backbone systems, video-conferencing centers, and satellite uplinks serving a business center that allows organizations to hold national board meetings on-line while in attendance at meetings in the facility. Seattle's SAFECO Field has installed a $1.9 million data and voice network designed by Lucent Technologies to handle day-to-day operations. Los Angeles's STAPLES Center was designed to accommodate two different sports (hockey and basketball) and four different home teams. The center was built with large storerooms on either side of the floor for bringing in and out team-logo floors, baskets, and other interchangeable fixtures. The stadium also utilizes articulated retractable seating sections to facilitate the switch from hockey to basketball and back again. These seats, appearing in more and more high-tech stadiums, maintain optimal sight lines for different sports and entertainment events without the necessity of physically removing entire seat sections. The seats can be raised or lowered for basketball or hockey and retracted for concerts and other special events.

Other architectural innovations that involve a marriage of art and technology include the intricately designed sight lines of AmericanAirlines Arena in Miami. New home of the NBA's Miami Heat, the arena has a "boxy" feel that connects the audience with the action.

From the concept stage to the grand opening, the architects, designers, planners, and contractors make the modern public assembly facility happen. Using more than 100 years of architectural and planning experience in designing stadiums, convention centers, arenas, auditoriums, and other public assembly facilities, today's architectural and planning firms draw upon the latest computerized technology to create facilities that incorporate both the past and the future in their designs.

ABOVE: A SYLVAN INDUSTRIES TECHNICIAN MEASURES ONE OF THE FIRM'S ARCHITECTURAL CONCRETE FORMS. VALUED FOR THEIR STRENGTH AND REFLECTIVE BEAUTY, THE FORMS ARE OFTEN USED IN ARENA CORRIDORS AND AISLES. LEFT: THE CEMENT MIXER ON THIS TRUCK HAS BEEN PAINTED TO LOOK LIKE A FOOTBALL, SUGGESTING TO PASSERSBY THAT STADIUM CONSTRUCTION IS A COMPANY SPECIALTY.

ARCHITECTS AND PLANNERS

FOUR
CORPORATE PROFILES

ARCHITECTS & PLANNERS

GEIGER ENGINEERS

Domes for more than one-third of the world's covered stadiums have been designed by Geiger Engineers—a leader in long span roofs and cable-supported dome technology.

With an international reputation for designing and engineering innovative long span roof systems, Geiger Engineers P.C. has been directly involved in creating many of the world's renowned arenas.

With its largest market in sports venues, the firm has been responsible for more than 100 of the world's arenas and stadiums, representing an impressive total of more than one million spectator seats worldwide. Domes for one-third of the world's covered stadiums are designs of Geiger Engineers.

The firm's impressive roster of engineering achievements is highly varied, and includes, for instance, floating marine structures as well as stage sets for live entertainment events.

Founded in 1988, Geiger Engineers evolved from a group of collaborative professionals who worked for more than 25 years under the tutelage of the firm's founder, the late David Geiger.

"David Geiger was a genius," says Paul Gossen, chief engineer and a principal in the firm. "He invented new structures and helped develop Teflon-coated fiberglass to cover them." Geiger's use of long span, cable dome designs set an industry standard. Geiger Engineers continues that legacy, establishing new industry benchmarks with aesthetically pleasing, economical designs for a variety of sports facility projects.

Headquartered in Suffern, New York, with an office in Bellingham, Washington, principals of Geiger Engineers have completed major projects across the United States as well as in England, Korea, Malaysia, Saudi Arabia, Japan, Taiwan, Republic of China, and Canada. This privately held firm employs 40 people and has annual sales of $4 million.

Geiger Engineers specializes in new design projects and renovation of spectator facilities. Specific building-type knowledge and familiarity with a broad assortment of conventional and nonconventional building materials enables the firm to address all types of assignments while, at the same time, achieving value and economy in structural design. Its strong commitment to innovative technologies has made it possible for many communities to have multiuse facilities—arenas able to house rock concerts as well as symphonies or basketball games—when a conventional approach would prove too costly.

Geiger Engineers continues on its path of imaginative design for the new millennium. Recent accomplishments include the creation of an innovative portable broadcast studio for the National Broadcasting Company to use in its coverage of the next five Olympic Games, beginning in Sydney, Australia, in 2000. Currently on the drawing board . . . the Seoul 2002 World Cup Stadium in Seoul, Korea, and the new St. Paul Minnesota arena for the NHL's Minnesota Wild.

Geiger Engineers designed and engineered the Crown Coliseum at Cumberland County Coliseum Complex, which opened in Fayetteville, North Carolina in 1997.

Geiger Engineers is also responsible for the BI-LO Center, in Greenville, South Carolina. The arena is the state's largest sports and entertainment facility.

THORNTON-TOMASETTI ENGINEERS
A DIVISION OF THE THORNTON-TOMASETTI GROUP INC.

THORNTON-TOMASETTI ENGINEERS IS A PREMIER STRUCTURAL ENGINEERING FIRM FOR MAJOR SPORTS FACILITIES AS WELL AS SIGNATURE BUILDING PROJECTS THROUGHOUT THE WORLD.

THORNTON-TOMASETTI PERFORMED THE STRUCTURAL ENGINEERING DESIGN FOR PHILIPS ARENA IN ATLANTA, GEORGIA. THE MAIN ENTRANCE ROOFS OF THIS STRUCTURE ARE SUPPORTED BY STRUCTURAL COLUMNS, RANGING FROM 25 TO 90 FEET TALL, THAT SPELL "ATLANTA." © RION RIZZO/CREATIVE SOURCES

From stadiums and arenas to exhibition halls and performing arts centers, Thornton-Tomasetti Engineers, a division of The Thornton-Tomasetti Group Inc., is recognized worldwide for its innovative structural engineering systems for building complexes.

Thornton-Tomasetti Engineers is renowned for providing aesthetic and functional design and engineering solutions tailored to meet the unique needs of each client and each project. The firm is acknowledged for its technical expertise and creativity in optimizing building systems to reduce costs, simplify erection procedures, and speed up construction.

"Historically, our approach has always been to innovate in order to meet a project's special needs, whether financial or functional," says Tom Scarangello, managing principal. "We work closely with the architectural design team to offer as many innovative alternatives as possible. This way, we assist them in arriving at the appropriate solution for a specific project." This approach has earned Thornton-Tomasetti numerous top-flight assignments and a reputation as a premier structural engineer for sports facilities in the United States. In the 1990s—with credits including Philips Arena in Atlanta, Georgia; Pepsi Center in Denver, Colorado; Adelphia Coliseum in Nashville, Tennessee; and AmericanAirlines Arena in Miami, Florida—the firm performed engineering design services for more than 30 sports teams, including 20 National Hockey League, National Basketball Association, Major League Baseball, and National Football League teams. Thornton-Tomasetti projects in the year 2000 include a covered stadium for Michigan's Detroit Lions, Pacific Bell Park for the San Francisco Giants and a new San Diego Padres ballpark in California, and the Nationwide Arena for the Columbus Blue Jackets in Ohio.

In addition to sports facilities, Thornton-Tomasetti has participated in such signature projects as the Petronas Twin Towers in Kuala Lumpur, Malaysia—to date, the tallest buildings in the world; the United Airlines terminal at Chicago O'Hare International Airport; Warburg Dillon Read headquarters in Stamford, Connecticut; two major high-rise buildings in New York City's Times Square; and numerous other commercial, institutional, and mixed-use developments. Through the years, Thornton Tomasetti Engineers has received hundreds of awards, and members of its staff have been rated among the "Top 25 Newsmakers" in *Engineering News-Record*.

The firm has offices in New York, New York; Newark, New Jersey; Trumbull, Connecticut; Boston, Massachusetts; Chicago, Illinois; Dallas, Texas; and Orange County, California.

Thornton-Tomasetti Engineers
A Division of The Thornton-Tomasetti Group

THORNTON-TOMASETTI PERFORMED THE STRUCTURAL DESIGN OF THE NEW $255-MILLION, 42,000-SEAT PACIFIC BELL PARK BASEBALL STADIUM. © LEN JOSEPH, THORNTON-TOMASETTI ENGINEERS

HOMASOTE COMPANY

HOMASOTE COMPANY SETS THE STANDARD FOR SOUND CONTROL IN FLOORS, CEILINGS, ROOFS, AND WALLS WITH ITS INNOVATIVE PRODUCTS MADE FROM RECYCLED MATERIALS.

The Homasote Company, named for its unique recycled and recyclable fiberboard, is the nation's oldest manufacturer of building products made from recycled paper.

The company was founded by Eugenius H. Outbridge in 1909 as the Agasote Millboard Company in West Trenton, New Jersey. His intention was to manufacture a high-density fiberboard utilizing a secret method he had purchased in England.

The unique fiberboard's first application was in the manufacture of roof panels for railroad passenger cars. In 1916 the fiberboard was used for automobile roofs. Success quickly followed as Agasote became a major producer for leading automakers.

Another milestone in 1916 came when the company debuted a strong yet lightweight weather-resistant product known as Homasote board. Because of its weather-resistant qualities, Homasote board was extremely useful. It was widely utilized in the construction of field facilities during World War I. Soon Homasote board was used for a variety of other applications and became the company's most versatile and popular product. As a result Agasote Millboard Company changed its name in 1936 to the Homasote Company.

Today the company has grown to be recognized all over the world, earning more than $30 million a year in sales. Its highly practical and innovative products are used for a variety of applications such as ice deck, a moisture-resistant structural panel that is used as a temporary cover over ice, artificial turf, gymnasium floors, and tennis courts; FireStall®, a structural roof decking; Homasote 440 Sound Barrier, a lightweight sound-deadening material; and Homex 300, a unique expansion joint and forming material.

The Homasote fiberboard products are environmentally safe, constructed entirely from post-consumer recycled waste paper. They contain no asbestos or formaldehyde additives. The structurally sound fiberboard acts as an insulator, boasting two to three times the strength of typical light-density wood fiberboard.

HOMASOTE HELPS CREATE A QUIET HOME. ABOVE: HOMASOTE PANELS REDUCE SOUND IMPACT AND TRANSMISSION IN FLOORS AND WALLS. LEFT: HOMASOTE 440 SOUND BARRIER IS LIGHTWEIGHT, STRUCTURAL SOUND-DEADENING MATERIAL THAT ACTS AS A REPLACEMENT FOR LIGHTWEIGHT CONCRETE, AT A FRACTION OF THE COST.

Homasote's manufacturing facility, encompassing 1,000,000 square feet, demonstrates conservation in action. With equipment running at full capacity approximately 300 tons of wastewater is recycled per day. In addition, the water removed from products during the manufacturing process is also recycled in a closed loop system, amounting to hundreds of thousands of gallons daily.

Employing nearly 250 people, the company is still located in West Trenton and is headed by Warren Flicker, CEO. Currently Homasote products are sold throughout the United States and Canada and are exported to more than 30 countries throughout the world.

FIRESTALL® ROOF DECKING WON'T FALL APART OR DELAMINATE AT TEMPERATURES ABOVE 130 DEGREES—TEMPERATURES THAT ARE COMMON IN ORDINARY ATTICS ON HOT DAYS. © J. GERARD SMITH

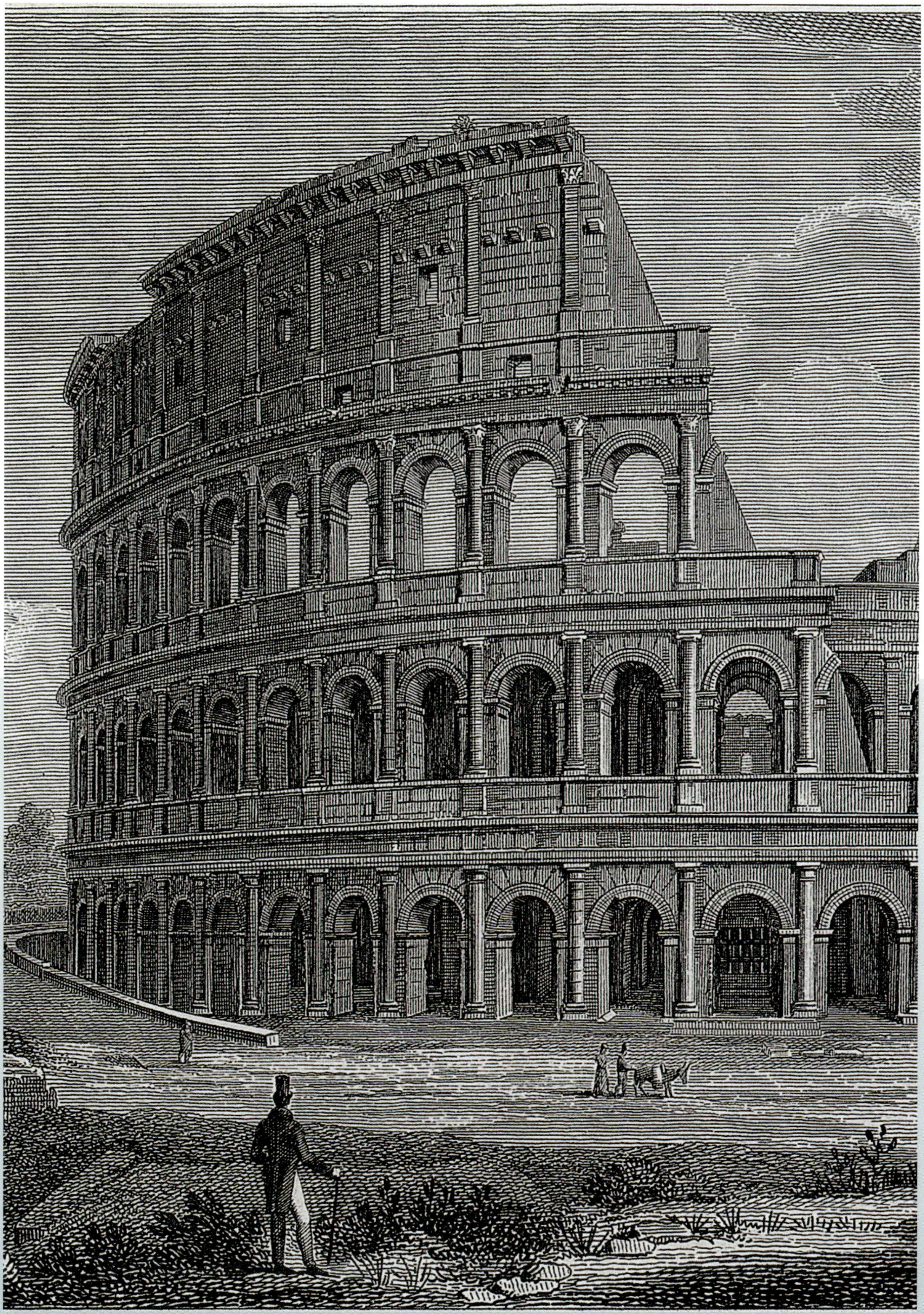

PHOTO: © BETTMANN/CORBIS

FIVE

BIG DEALS:
CREATIVE FUNDING FOR PUBLIC FACILITIES

COMMUNITIES ACROSS AMERICA HAVE ALWAYS USED CREATIVE FUNDING MECHANISMS TO BUILD PUBLIC ASSEMBLY FACILITIES AND SUPPORT THE ENTERTAINMENT VENUES THAT CALL THOSE

ABOVE: BASEBALL COMMISSIONER KENESAW MOUNTAIN LANDIS (LEFT) SHAKES HANDS WITH COLONEL JACOB RUPPERT, OWNER OF THE NEW YORK YANKEES, AT THE 1923 WORLD SERIES IN YANKEE STADIUM. OPPOSITE: LIGHT SCULPTURES ENHANCE THE LOOK OF LOS ANGELES'S STAPLES CENTER, DESIGNED BY NBBJ ARCHITECTS. THE $375 MILLION ARENA WAS BUILT WITH $58.5 MILLION IN PUBLIC FUNDS, THE REMAINDER SUPPLIED BY THE TEAMS. STAPLES, INC., WILL PAY $116 MILLION OVER 20 YEARS FOR NAMING RIGHTS.

facilities home. In the early days of the industry, entrepreneurs and businesspeople often built sports stadiums to house their teams; Colonel Jacob Ruppert of the New York Yankees helped pioneer the concept when he built Yankee Stadium to showcase the talents of Babe Ruth and the Bronx Bombers in the early 1920s.

Through the 1950s and 1960s, cities and towns often used bond issues to help build coliseums, stadiums, and convention centers. During the Great Depression, the federal Public Works Administration (PWA) helped a number of communities build coliseums for their state fairgrounds. In the boom years following World War II, U.S. cities used their favorable bond ratings to build hundreds of public assembly facilities. The explosion of interest in professional sports from the mid-1960s to the mid-1980s made it easy to finance stadiums and arenas. Municipalities discovered that they could bring in additional revenue to help pay off general obligation bonds by leasing their facilities for rock concerts and touring performances of popular artists. These events also had the potential to generate revenues that could be used by the city for other purposes.

From the PAF manager's perspective, things began to change for the worse in the 1970s. With the advent of Arab oil embargoes, rising interest rates began to preclude the easy placement of municipal bond issues. And the passage of the Deficit Reduction Act of 1984 and the Tax Reform Act of 1986 made it much more difficult for communities to finance public assembly facilities with tax-exempt bonds.

PUBLIC/PRIVATE PARTNERSHIPS

In the 1980s and 1990s, the trend of financing public assembly facilities reverted back to participation by the private sector, and that trend continues today. Communities still build stadiums, arenas, performing arts centers, and amphitheaters, but increasingly, entrepreneurs—especially in the big-time world of professional sports—are partners with their host communities in the construction of stadiums, ballparks, and arenas.

69

FIVE

Municipal governments in this new phenomenon of public/private partnership can bring many things to the table, including land, public capital revenue streams, condemnation authority, infrastructure improvements, and tax abatements. Private sector partners likewise can sweeten a deal with investment capital, acceptance of risk, operating knowledge, and tenants. However the deal is structured, public-private partnerships are often a win-win situation for all involved.

Since the passage of tax reform legislation in the mid-1980s, municipalities and their private sector partners have become far more sophisticated in the kinds of financial instruments they use to build new public assembly facilities. Lease-backed financing helps a convention or sports authority benefit from the credit strength of a municipal or local government while establishing specific rental payments to service debt. Special tax district bonds allow the authority and its private sector tenants to apply expected property tax assessments to debt service. Certificates of participation, while often carrying higher interest rates than traditional obligation bonds, have become a popular instrument for financing sports facilities. Since the sponsoring government entity is not legally committed to repay the certificates, certificates have the advantage of not requiring voter approval for issuance. This gives both the holders and the issuing authority more flexibility and less financial risk.

ABOVE: FORMERLY KNOWN AS RIVERFRONT STADIUM, CINCINNATI'S CINERGY FIELD WAS RENAMED IN 1996. RIGHT: ANAHEIM CONVENTION CENTER IN ORANGE COUNTY, CALIFORNIA, IS UNDERGOING A 40 PERCENT EXPANSION AS PART OF THE ANAHEIM RESORT PROJECT. MORE THAN $4 BILLION IN IMPROVEMENTS TO THE CITY ARE EXPECTED THROUGH PUBLIC AND PRIVATE FUNDS BY 2005.

NAMING RIGHTS

One of the newest trends in the industry involves the purchase of naming rights for public assembly facilities by America's corporations. Insurance companies such as SAFECO and Conseco, utilities such as Cinergy and Xcel Energy, consumer companies such as Coors, and technology companies such as RCA and 3Com have found that putting their name on a public assembly facility is a surefire way to keep their name in front of millions of people each year.

Naming rights are big business. The Bonham Group, a Denver-based sports marketing firm, estimated in 1999 that there were 48 naming rights agreements in place at North American stadiums and arenas, with a total value of more than $1.4 billion. Naming rights can mean the difference between profit and loss for a new public assembly facility, and many agreements specify operations and maintenance payments well into the future. When the city of Houston negotiated a naming rights agreement with computer

BIG DEALS

SHOPS AND CONCESSIONS AT HOUSTON'S COMPAQ CENTER REFLECT THE STADIUM'S UPDATED DESIGN. CHANGES UNDER WAY INCLUDE NEW SEATS, NEW SIGNS, NEW SCOREBOARDS, NEW LIGHTS, AND A NEW SOUND SYSTEM FOR THIS HOME OF FOUR MAJOR SPORTS TEAMS.

giant Compaq, provisions required the company to pay $900,000 a year for maintenance and renovations of the Compaq Center.

Sports arenas and stadiums aren't the only facilities to benefit from naming rights. Increasingly, civic and convention center managers are seeking partners when they announce plans to build a new facility. When the Wisconsin Center District embarked upon planning for its new convention center, its leaders approached Midwest Express Airlines about participating. The result was the Midwest Express Center, which the regional air carrier agreed to support to the tune of $9.25 million over 15 years.

ADDED ATTRACTIONS

Municipalities and public-private partners in the world of professional

GIVING BACK TO THE COMMUNITY

The Indiana Convention Center in Indianapolis is perhaps the only convention center in the nation to draw upon private money for its construction needs. When the city's Capital Improvement Board announced plans for a 100,000-square-foot expansion of the facility in 1997, its members approached the hometown Lilly Endowment for help with underwriting the $45 million job. • Founded in 1937 and funded by stock from the Indianapolis-based pharmaceutical firm Eli Lilly & Company, the endowment is among the nation's largest. One of its longtime missions is to help foster the civic and cultural life of its hometown. The endowment board readily agreed to make a grant for $30 million for the convention center expansion. For its part, the city financed the balance with a one percent hotel-motel tax. • A portion of the Lilly Endowment grant—$1.5 million—was earmarked for a local public-private partnership set up to help train residents of the inner city for jobs in the hotel and tourism industry.

CREATIVE FUNDING FOR PUBLIC FACILITIES

FIVE

72

Big Deals

LEFT: AMERICANAIRLINES ARENA IN MIAMI IS THE RESULT OF INNOVATIVE PARTNERING BETWEEN PUBLIC, TEAM, AND CORPORATE INTERESTS. OPPOSITE: SEATTLE STORM CENTER SIMONE EDWARDS TAKES MOMENTARY CONTROL AGAINST THE LOS ANGELES SPARKS AT SEATTLE'S KEY ARENA DURING THE 2000 WNBA SEASON. WOMEN'S BASKETBALL IS ONE OF MANY ATTRACTIONS RECENTLY ADDED TO FILL U.S. STADIUM SEATS.

sports have also discovered that perquisites can be a lucrative way to help pay off the mortgage on stadiums and arenas. Luxury suites can command as much as $1 million in additional revenues every year. Also known as skyboxes, corporate suites, or executive suites, luxury suites are enclosed areas surrounding the arena or stadium that seat eight people or more.

Premium and club seating, along with seat licensing deals, are another facet of alternate revenue streams for public assembly facilities. Club seats are typically cushioned, and seat licenses guarantee season-ticket holders the same seat for a specified period of time. Projected revenue from luxury suites and seat licenses can often actually finance construction of a stadium or arena. When the ALLTEL Arena opened in Little Rock late in 1999, the 26 luxury suites in the facility meant $10 million in income to the arena.

Of course, corporate patrons who are spending $1 million a year for a luxury suite expect a little more than hot dogs and stadium parking. It's no wonder that builders of Los Angeles's STAPLES Center added the Arena Club, a 500-seat restaurant overlooking the court, to cater to wealthy owners of luxury suites and holders of premium seats. Suite holders at the Hubert Humphrey Metrodome in Minneapolis are invited to autograph sessions with active and retired players; suite holders at the Target Center across town get free health club memberships.

And most cities that have helped finance major league sports facilities manage to negotiate a share of revenue each game day.

HOT FINANCING

AmericanAirlines Arena, the new home of the Miami Heat NBA basketball team, represents an interesting public-private financing arrangement. Land for the facility, valued at $34 million, was donated by Miami-Dade county, which owns the building and collects 5 percent of ticket sales as rent and $100,000 a year in naming rights. American Airlines will contribute $2.1 million a year for 20 years for those rights. Other corporate sponsorships total an additional $14 million a year. • The Miami Heat raised $185 million in corporate bonds towards construction, and the team itself serves as collateral. Micky Arison, owner of the Heat, put up $40 million of his own to guarantee the bonds. In return, the team keeps 95 percent of arena ticket monies from team games. The Heat also keeps profits from concessions and rents paid by other tenants, such as concert bands. • The city of Miami helps with operations, giving up $6.4 million a year from its hotel tax income. • This participation among city, county, sports, and corporate investors has resulted in an exciting new venue that promises to breathe new life into downtown Miami.

CREATIVE FUNDING FOR PUBLIC FACILITIES

That means that a city whose team makes a run deep into the play-offs can expect a revenue windfall. When the Indianapolis Colts unexpectedly ran away with the American Football Conference East championship in 1999 and hosted a January 2000 play-off game at the city-owned RCA Dome, Indianapolis taxpayers shared in their team's good fortune. Since the city has negotiated a percentage cut on each ticket and hot dog sold each game, the $3 million in ticket sales and $550,000 in concession sales on play-off game day translated to an extra $155,500 for the city of Indianapolis to add to bond payments.

Better to Be in the Red Than 'in the Black'

As far back as 30 years ago, the IAAM made an observation about the financial performance of public assembly facilities that is as true today as it was then.

"For an auditorium to finish its budget year in the red is not at all embarrassing, if that auditorium has served its community well and filled a real community need," noted Charles Byrnes, then the executive director of IAAM. "To be in the red is not as embarrassing as to be 'in the black.' Darkened or idle from nonuse, a community resource like an auditorium has no value to it."

Byrnes went on to explain that the number one problem of the PAF manager was to convince his or her community to use, and assist in using, its auditorium resource to the maximum of its potential. "An auditorium," he wrote, "should be as valuable to its community as possible by simply becoming a part of the important decisions regarding its future and the enjoyment of it by its citizens."

Byrnes's observation is key to understanding the financial pressures that most PAF managers face when explaining a facility's importance to the community and assisting city officers in deciding whether to build or expand. Even if the new facility looks like a money loser in the beginning, it might well become a bargain for the community if it is in constant use for several years.

PAF managers have long realized the financial benefit of multiuse facilities. While professional or collegiate sports tenants may provide the bulk of the revenue for most stadiums and arenas, PAF managers rely on nonanchor events to help reach financial goals. Concerts, family shows, and motor sports events are most frequently the attractions by which public assembly facilities increase their diversity of use and financial return.

In a recent study, professional stadium managers reported that their facilities drew an average of 31,800 patrons for nonanchor concerts and 33,000 patrons for motor sports events. Professional arena managers reported that they averaged an attendance of 11,700 people for concerts and 8,400 people for family shows such as circuses and ice-skating exhibitions. Arenas in the National Collegiate Athletic Association (NCAA) attracted an average of 4,000 people for both concerts and family shows.

The trend towards multiuse of facilities is best illustrated in the world of ice hockey. Several generations of PAF managers could tell horror stories about putting down ice sheets in the 1930s and 1940s at their facilities for touring ice hockey and ice-skating exhibitions. Once relegated to ice-bound Canadian and northern U.S. communities, today ice hockey has spurred a major increase in the development of ice sheets for

ABOVE: CENTURIES-OLD LACROSSE HAS A HEALTHY MODERN FOLLOWING. OPPOSITE: A VALUABLE COMMUNITY RESOURCE, COLORADO SPRINGS' WORLD ARENA OFFERS ICE SPORTS FACILITIES TO COLLEGE AND YOUTH HOCKEY TEAMS, ASPIRING FIGURE SKATERS, AND THE PUBLIC.

participatory activities by youth and adult hockey leagues nationwide. In fact, ice hockey may be the fastest-growing professional and minor league sport in North America. A whopping 60 percent of arenas nationwide now have ice capabilities.

Sports such as arena football, indoor soccer, and women's basketball are also gaining ground in multiuse facilities. The $110 million New Orleans Arena opened next to the Louisiana Superdome in October 1999 as home of the New Orleans Brass hockey team, but with plans to host the Tulane University Green Wave basketball team and an Arena Football League team as well. Boasting a seating plan that ranges from 13,000 to 19,000 seats, the New Orleans facility was built to also accommodate concerts, festivals, family shows, banquets and other private parties, trade shows and exhibits, Mardi Gras parties, closed-circuit television presentations, and ancillary activities for major conventions. Sized larger than existing arenas in the region, but smaller and more intimate than the 70,000-seat Superdome, the New Orleans Arena is considered the perfect size for the variety of events planned.

Even smaller facilities without a sports team attached can offer enough variety in entertainment to justify the investment made in them. Take, for example, Mississippi's new 2,000 to 6,000-seat Tunica Arena and Exposition Center. The $20 million center was built to provide a wider choice of entertainment in what is becoming a major gaming destination in the United States. Tunica's 10 casinos entertain close to one million visitors a year, visitors who want other activities to round out their vacations. The county owners of the property also saw the potential to draw more conventions to their area. Hence, the Tunica Arena and Exposition Center can handle everything from trade shows to car shows to "dirt shows" (such as rodeos and tractor pulls) to ice shows.

Public assembly facilities that are adaptable to multiuse purposes increase revenue streams, and as managers continue to look for ways to remain financially competitive,

CREATIVE FUNDING FOR PUBLIC FACILITIES

the trend will likely continue and accelerate. Already, naming rights sales and seat licensing—trends that became common among professional sports assembly facilities during the 1990s—are getting more common on college campuses.

Universities still rely on the time-honored practice of large donations from alumni to help fund arenas and performing arts centers, such as the Burtness Theatre at the University of North Dakota. But alumni donations and naming rights are increasingly blurred. The University of Wisconsin's Kohl Center honors the major grant from a Badger State business executive and U.S. senator. The new Value City Arena at the Jerome Schottenstein Center at Ohio State University and the United Spirit Arena (named for United Supermarkets) at Texas Tech University further illustrate how naming rights have made inroads on college campuses in recent years.

And facility managers at Pennsylvania State University with its renovation of Beaver Stadium, University of Alabama with its renovation of Bryant-Denny Stadium, University of Texas with its renovation of Darrell K. Royal Memorial Stadium, and Louisiana State University with its renovation of Tiger Stadium have all realized the financial importance of season seat licensing as a part of their stadium renovation programs.

Funding the Performing Arts

To a certain extent, the public assembly facility industry and sports have been intertwined for much of the 20th century. And the explosion in the popularity of professional sports in the past quarter-century—fueled in part by television revenues—has, to a certain extent, provided a financial safety net for PAF managers lucky enough to have a professional sports team as a tenant.

But what about the arts? Performing arts centers, amphitheaters, and auditoriums offer a wide variety of entertainment, including symphony orchestras, touring Broadway shows, dance troupes, and repertory theater—attractions that don't always generate substantial profit on ticket sales alone.

THE JOHN F. KENNEDY CENTER FOR THE PERFORMING ARTS IN WASHINGTON, D.C., HELPS FUND NATIONWIDE DEVELOPMENT OF NEW THEATER WORKS FOR ADULT, YOUTH, AND UNIVERSITY AUDIENCES, AS WELL AS ARTS EDUCATION AND OUTREACH. SHOWN IS THE JFK BUST IN THE LOBBY.

Fortunately, the arts have funding mechanisms that help them survive and sometimes even thrive in today's competitive entertainment marketplace. The federal government has long recognized the unique place that the arts play in our cultural lives, and the National Endowment for the Arts (NEA) annually makes hundreds of millions of dollars in grants available to the arts community. Most of the grants require a match from the recipient organization. Roughly 35 percent of NEA grants go directly to state arts agencies.

State arts agencies, which get an average of 72 percent of their

Big Deals

funding from their state legislatures, help to subsidize many of the tenants of performing arts centers, amphitheaters, and auditoriums. New York, Michigan, and California traditionally lead the nation in state support of the arts, while Hawaii ranks first in the nation in per capita spending.

The arts community has been innovative in its approach to public and private funding. In the 1990s, 28 states came up with a host of alternative funding mechanisms to help support the arts, including endowment funds, tax exempt bond issues, lotteries, license plate programs, state income tax check-offs, corporate filing fees, special tax districts, and local option taxes earmarked for the arts. Like their counterparts in the business of sports, savvy arts managers are even beginning to offer seat licensing programs for holders of season tickets to symphony orchestras, choral groups, and repertory theaters.

University performing arts center managers have become particularly adept at maximizing revenue sources. Most university centers are partly supported by student fees, but those fees often don't cover operating costs. University center managers in recent years have turned to corporate sponsorships, series subscriptions, special memberships, and merchandising in order to help offset annual operating expenses.

Arts groups often have to walk a fine line when it comes to expenses for the public assembly facilities that host their group. The performing arts theater manager is there because he or she truly loves the arts. But the facility manager is beholden to a municipal authority; a university board of regents; or a private, not-for-profit arts corporation that must look to the bottom line. Maintaining financial and programming viability requires the facility manager to forge a partnership with his or her arts group tenants to search for new ideas and initiatives to ensure both top-quality programming and financial health.

Paying to build and maintain public assembly facilities has been an exercise in creativity and innovation that has lasted throughout the 20th century. Those creative and innovative approaches are likely to continue as the industry embarks on a new century.

ABOVE: THE KANSAS CITY BALLET HAS BEEN ENTERTAINING DANCE LOVERS FOR NEARLY 50 YEARS. FACED WITH EXTINCTION IN THE EARLY 1990S, THE COMPANY RAISED MONEY TO PAY OFF DEBTS, STRENGTHENED ITS ENDOWMENT, UPGRADED PRODUCTIONS, AND MOVED TO A NEW VENUE. LEFT: COUNTRY MUSIC FANS ENJOY A CONCERT AT PHELPS STOKES CHAPEL, BEREA COLLEGE, KENTUCKY.

CREATIVE FUNDING FOR PUBLIC FACILITIES

SIX

Innovative Thinking: Operations and Equipment

Public assembly facilities are bricks and mortar, concrete and steel, wood and glass. They are also a product of the hundreds of people whose efforts ensure that all who attend an entertainment or sporting event have the safe and clean environment they are entitled to with the purchase of a ticket.

One doesn't necessarily think of that when the Columbus Symphony Orchestra crescendos into the final movement of Richard Wagner's *Tristan und Isolde,* or when Dan Marino directs the Miami Dolphins on one of their patented game-winning drives in the final minutes against the Buffalo Bills. But for every entertainment and sporting event, there are many workers behind the scenes creating the illusion that people have paid to see.

The People

The facility itself requires hundreds of hours of maintenance each week. People clean the restrooms and make sure that the heating, ventilation, and air-conditioning systems are working at peak performance. Seating needs to be attended to, and a small army of workers cleans the aisles and concourses before and after each event.

A stage performance or concert requires the attention of dozens of stagehands, lighting crew, and sound technicians. Stages, sound and light systems, TV hookups, dressing rooms, signs, and other facilities for the performers and crew may need to be loaded in and set up or adapted to the show.

If one is watching a sporting event, then a facilities crew has been on the field or court or rink to ensure that it is in top playing condition. In a natural grass stadium, groundskeepers groom the field and check the irrigation system. In a stadium with artificial turf, specialists constantly replace and repair the synthetic turf and check that padding and seams are all in place. Ice hockey arena maintenance workers have a full-time job ensuring that refrigeration and piping systems work as they should.

For any performance or sporting event, tickets have to be

Above: A television director and technician monitor their broadcast from the studio. They are two of many behind-the-scenes crews whose efforts ensure a positive—and profitable—experience. Broadcasting sporting events live has become an expected part of a big game. Opposite: In the spring of 1949, 16-year-old trained vendor Patrick Giblin hawks fresh, hot peanuts over the roar of the crowd in Yankee Stadium.

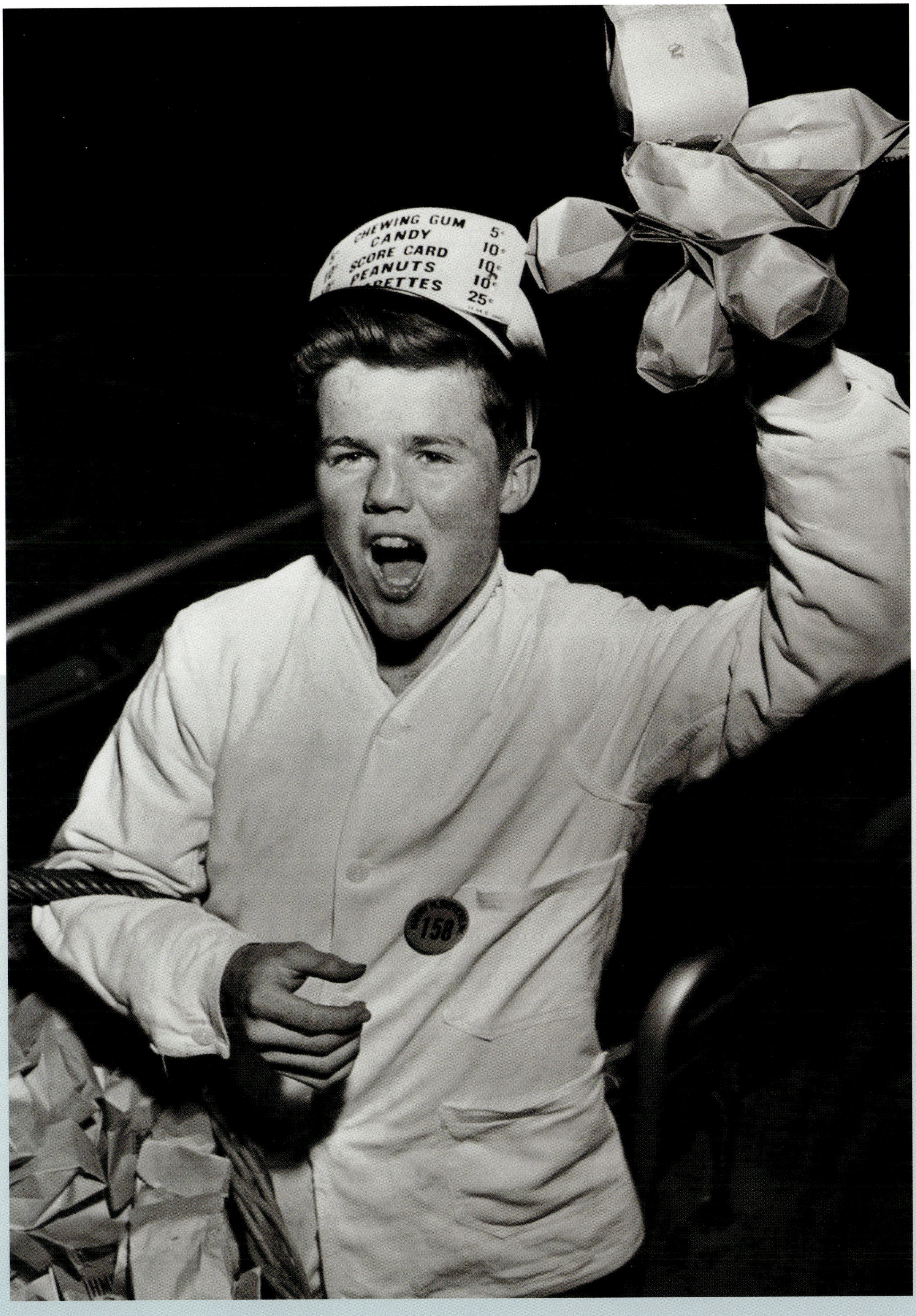
CHEWING GUM 5¢
CANDY 10¢
SCORE CARD 10¢
PEANUTS 10¢
25¢
158

printed, sold, and taken at the gate. Concessions must be stocked and staffed and, where food and drink are involved, must comply to regulations. Crowd control, parking, and traffic issues involve careful planning, maintenance, and training of employees. Every public assembly facility manager in America understands the importance of customer service, and a legion of ushers, food service workers, and security personnel strive to make every performance, every event, an experience to savor and remember.

It is the public assembly facility manager's job to make sure that the processes are in place to make all this happen successfully. The PAF manager not only supervises the services that affect the audience directly, but settles with the promoter; meets with accountants, consultants, and attorneys; deals with unions and regulatory issues affecting workers; evaluates and purchases insurance; prepares the facility for emergency situations where evacuation is necessary; and performs a host of other critical functions. In addition to day-to-day operations, the PAF manager may, for example, meet with consultants to go over a marketing plan for the newly renovated suites on the upper concourse of the arena. Once that marketing plan is in place, the new suites must be relentlessly promoted, along with the arena's other attractions. And the responsibility for advertising and promotion again rests with the PAF manager.

Sales, marketing, community relations, event programming, strategic planning—all fall under the PAF manager's job description, as well as fiscal planning, management, and accountability.

Under constant scrutiny by the public, the community, and the sports and entertainment entities that use them, public assembly facilities must deliver the goods time after time. Perhaps that is why public assembly facility managers are in the vanguard when it comes to finding innovative ways to operate and adapt to the special needs of large-scale public gatherings.

THE LITTLE THINGS IN LIFE

One example of innovative thinking when it comes to public assembly facilities is an unlikely invention by an Italian-American entrepreneur named Frank Zamboni. With his two brothers, Zamboni moved to California in 1922 and soon after opened an electrical business that targeted the state's dairy industry. The three Zambonis then got involved in refrigeration for the

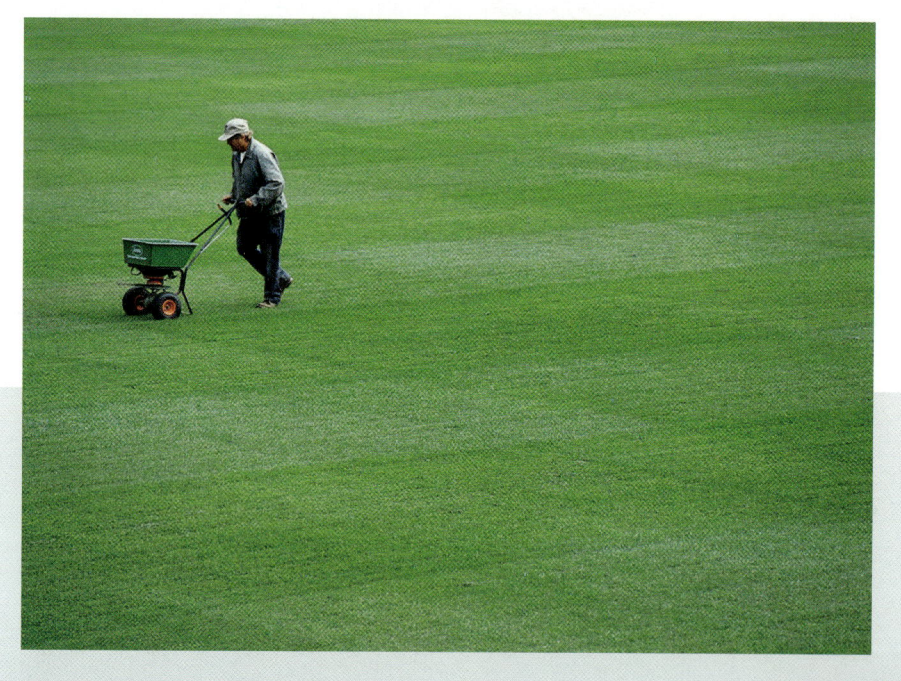

ABOVE: THE FIELD AT NOTRE DAME STADIUM IN SOUTH BEND, INDIANA, IS GROOMED BEFORE A BIG GAME. NOTRE DAME WAS RANKED AMONG THE WORLD'S TOP 20 SPORTING VENUES OF THE 20TH CENTURY BY SPORTS ILLUSTRATED MAGAZINE. RIGHT: GROUNDSKEEPER JOHN GODFREY SETS HOME PLATE FOR THE PHILADELPHIA PHILLIES' OPENING DAY 1963 IN CONNIE MACK STADIUM.

INNOVATIVE THINKING

In this 1985 photo, Frank Zamboni stands in front of the ice resurfacing machine he invented in the 1940s. Today, "Zambonis" are used in ice rinks around the world.

booming California produce market, and began making block ice for customers who wanted to ship their produce east.

In 1939, the Zambonis built a skating rink at Paramount, California. Grooming the ice was a time-consuming task involving a tractor pulling a scraper. Once the ice was shaved, workers had to spray water on the surface, squeegee it nearly dry, and wait for a thin layer of water to freeze on the surface. Resurfacing the ice often took an hour or more.

Frank Zamboni came up with a machine that vastly simplified the task of shaving the ice, and shortened grooming time to minutes instead of hours. The four-wheel Zamboni has become well-known nationally, appearing in Charles Schultz's *Peanuts* comic strip and even in the lyrics to popular songs.

That first Zamboni came out of the shop in 1949, and worked in much the same way as the Zamboni of today. A blade mounted under the driver's seat shaves the ice, which is then conveyed to a snow tank in the front of the machine. Meanwhile, water is fed from a wash-water tank at the driver's right hand to a squeegee-like conditioner behind the blade. The dirty water is vacuumed and returned to the tank, while a thin layer of clean, hot water is spread on the ice by a towel behind the conditioner.

In the 50 years since Frank Zamboni lent his name to one of the more innovative pieces of equipment still in use, more than 6,500 Zambonis have rolled out of the company's California and Ontario factories.

For patrons of ice hockey, and for ice-skating participants, Zamboni may be a household name. But how many patrons of the myriad of sports and entertainment venues ever give much thought to the other equipment that makes their attendance so enjoyable?

Take chairs, for example. Every public assembly facility in the world is equipped with chairs, from the plush seating in luxury boxes at stadiums and arenas to the ubiquitous metal folding chair utilized by convention and civic centers.

Sight lines, comfort, safety, appearance, and cost are the five major factors dictating selection of seating for a public assembly

OPERATIONS AND EQUIPMENT

82

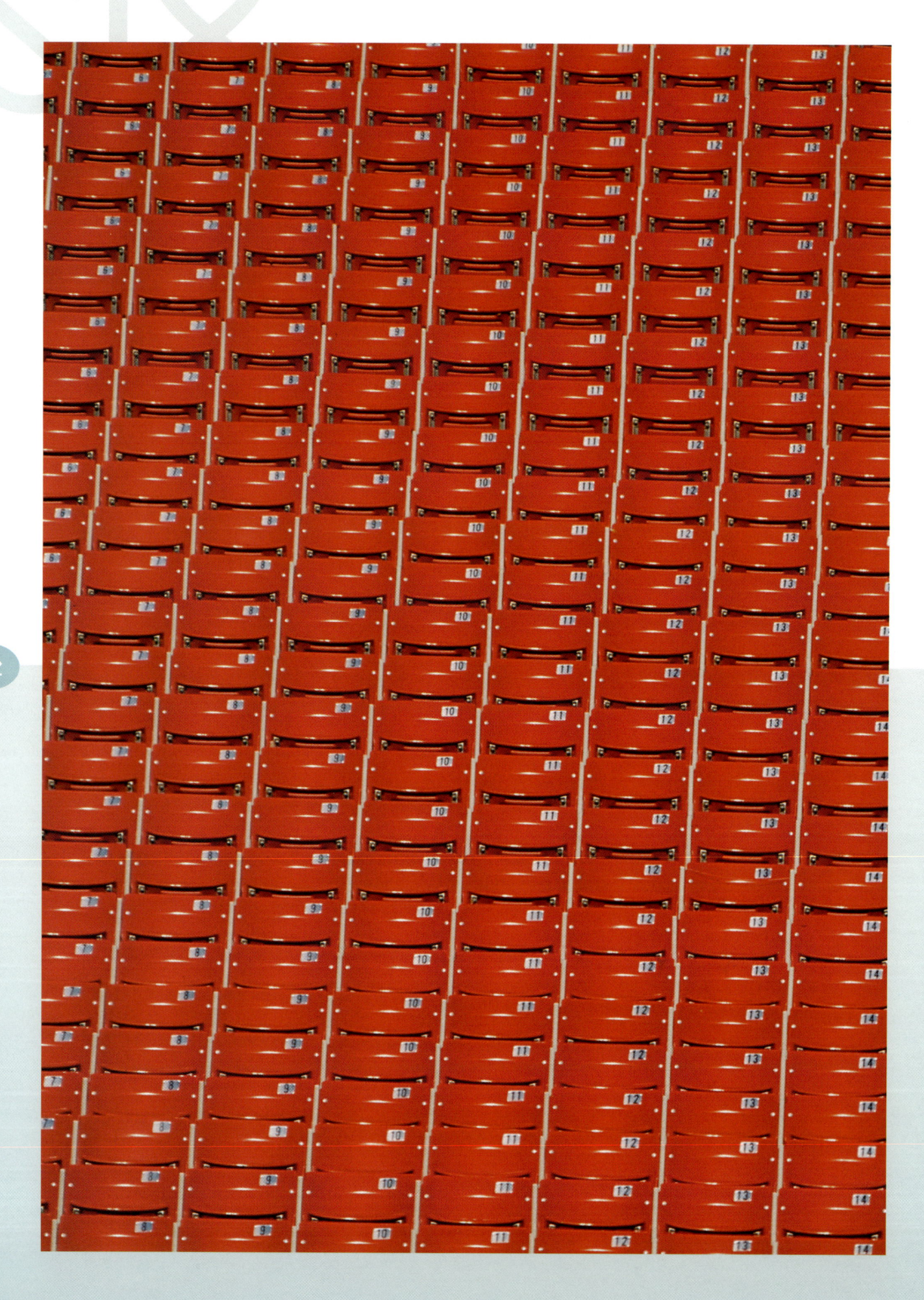

INNOVATIVE THINKING

LEFT: THREE THOUSAND CLARIN FOLDING CHAIRS ARE SET IN METICULOUS ROWS FOR AN EARLY-20TH-CENTURY BOXING MATCH AT THE CHICAGO HIPPODROME. OPPOSITE: COLORADO'S MILE HIGH STADIUM IN DENVER, WHICH HOSTED THE 1995 OLYMPIC FESTIVAL, BOASTS 76,098 SEATS, INCLUDING THIS SEEMINGLY ENDLESS BANK OF FIXED FOLDING CHAIRS.

facility. Bleacher seating, telescopic seating, and portable seating are the most common types of seating available in today's modern public assembly facility.

Perhaps the biggest innovations in public assembly facility seating during the past decade have been made to accommodate individuals with physical disabilities under the terms of the Americans with Disabilities Act. Literally every public assembly facility in America today makes provisions to include wheelchair boxes with adequate sight lines and easy access.

In 1923, inventor Werner Clarin created and patented the design for the X-frame metal folding chair that is a staple in many stadiums, arenas, convention centers, and other meeting facilities in America. Fans attending events at the STAPLES Center in Los Angeles, the Raymond James Stadium in Tampa, the Compaq Center in Houston, the Schottenstein Center at Ohio State University, and hundreds of other public assembly facilities are sitting on Clarin chairs. Likewise, attendees at conventions at the Northern Kentucky Convention Center, the Tucson Convention Center, the Hartford Civic Center, the Springfield Civic Center, and dozens of other civic and convention centers are sitting comfortably through presentations and seminars, thanks to Clarin chairs.

Southern California–based industry giant Virco has established a strong presence in the arena and convention center marketplace. Virco started out making chairs and desks for Los Angeles schools over 50 years ago, but soon grew to supply the hospitality, food services, and public assembly markets. The company recently won a design award at NeoCon 99, a major contract furniture trade show.

One of the nation's major makers of stadium and university seating is KI, a Green Bay, Wisconsin, manufacturer. With facilities in Wisconsin and Mississippi in the United States and in Ontario, Canada, KI specializes in serving the university arena seating market. Its Front Row Seating line displays a school's insignia or mascot and includes vinyl upholstered seats or upholstered seats and backrests.

WEBCASTING ON THE RISE

Internet viewers of the 1999 World Series could pick their shots, literally, using telerobotic cameras stationed in Atlanta's Turner Field and New York's Yankee Stadium. Perceptual Robotics (PRI) provided the means to Webcast this event and others, such as the 2000 *Grammy Awards*, through its TrueLook system for live visual telepresence. Using PRI iCams, viewers can zoom in on action in the field and take on-line snapshots to send to friends. More and more public assembly facilities are availing themselves of Webcasting technology, and as bandwidth and related technologies expand, so will Webcasting's uses and market potential.

OPERATIONS AND EQUIPMENT

Irwin Seating Company of Grand Rapids, Michigan, is the world's largest manufacturer of public seating for movie theaters, auditoriums, arenas, performing arts centers, and convention centers. Irwin Seats are established in venues around the world, from the Festival Hall in Osaka, Japan, to Carnegie Hall in New York City.

Other companies, such as American Seating Company of Grand Rapids, Michigan, make fans and patrons comfortable at such venues as New York's Radio City Music Hall, Wrigley Field in Chicago, and Comerica Park in Detroit.

Or take signage. How many fans at major sporting events take for granted the electronic displays that keep them updated on the progress of the event? Daktronics Inc., founded in 1968 by two electrical engineering professors in the tiny community of Brookings, South Dakota, helps fans at sporting events around the world keep track of what is happening on the field, the court, the rink, or the track.

The technology-driven company provides and installs some of the largest full-color video screens in the world. When 400,000 fans at the Indianapolis 500 in May 2000 wanted to know who was on the lead lap late in the race, they checked one of the seven large Daktronics video screens placed strategically around the two-and-one-half-mile oval. Baseball fans at Seattle's SAFECO Field can watch video replays and stay up-to-date with a variety of statistics, including pitch speed and type. It's a far cry from the days when a pair of youngsters manually updated the center field scoreboard in America's baseball parks.

Chicago-based White Way Sign Company is another major player in the signage industry. White Way specializes in sports and commercial signage and manufactured electronically controlled scoreboards, message centers, and building marquees. Fans at the Alamodome in San Antonio, Comiskey Park in Chicago, the Jacksonville Coliseum, and dozens of other major league stadiums and arenas get their scores, statistics, and replays from White Way Signs.

One of Oregon's fastest growing companies, Clarity Visual Systems is pioneering new approaches to liquid crystal display (LCD) sign technology. Based in the Portland suburb of Wilsonville, Clarity has branched out since its founding in 1995 from its initial base in education to providing a broad variety of large-screen technologies to the entertainment and retail industries. Clarity's latest coup involved a January 2000 joint venture with Siren Technologies to install a Digital Menuboard in London's Millennium Dome.

Innovative thinking in public assembly facility design and operation has led to a host of inventions that have found adaptations in everyday life. In the 1950s,

BELOW, LEFT: STADIUM SIGNAGE FEATURING LIVE-ACTION IMAGES AND RAPIDLY UPDATING STATISTICS IS USED IN PLACES SUCH AS RAYMOND JAMES STADIUM IN TAMPA, FLORIDA. BELOW, RIGHT: BIG SCREENS GIVE EVERYONE A FRONT-ROW SEAT AT THE INDIANAPOLIS MOTOR SPEEDWAY.

Chemstrand, a Monsanto subsidiary, experimented with a synthetic grass carpeting that could be used for outdoor sports facilities. The first artificial turf in use anywhere in the world was installed late that decade on a Providence, Rhode Island, high school football field.

It wasn't until five years later that the name AstroTurf entered the language, when Monsanto laid down synthetic carpeting in the Houston Astrodome, the world's first domed stadium. Composed of nylon, polypropylene, urethane, or other plastic, the synthetic turf, in widespread use for field sports around the world, is laid on a rubberized padding over a sand-gravel-asphalt base. Many fans go home from an athletic contest played on artificial turf to a patio or yard enclosure covered in a variation of synthetic turf.

RED SOX FANS STILL GET THEIR STATS THE OLD-FASHIONED WAY IN BOSTON'S FENWAY PARK. THAT'S 18-YEAR-OLD JOHN STONE KEEPING SCORE IN 1986. JOHN STANDS IN A ROOM WHERE THE WALLS ARE COVERED WITH SIGNATURES OF BALLPLAYERS WHO HAVE PLAYED AT FENWAY.

Multipurpose public assembly facilities depend on a wide variety of building configurations to maximize the community's investment in the facility. Seating, signage, and floor coverings, as well as various tables, platforms, and acoustical divider panels, appear in innumerable combinations throughout the public assembly industry. These permanent, semipermanent, and portable fixtures make it possible for an ice show, a sales and marketing seminar, a rock concert, and a trade show to be held in the same building within days of one another.

FEEDING THE MASSES

For most people, entertainment and food are linked. Whether it's a black-tie symphony affair; a family trip to the ball game; or a boat, sports, or travel show, the public expects to be fed.

In the early days of the industry, the gustatory fare was pretty simple. Legend has it that one afternoon in 1902, Harry M. Stevens, a food service vendor at the Polo Grounds in New York City, had the bright idea of stuffing a sausage into a long roll to fill the appetite of hungry New York Giants fans. Baseball fans could take their hot dogs plain or slathered with mustard and onions. Popcorn has also been a staple since early in the 20th century. Salted-in-the-shell peanuts and Cracker Jacks—caramel-coated popcorn and peanuts—have been favorite snacks since the late 19th century.

OPERATIONS AND EQUIPMENT

SIX

And what sporting event would be complete without a cold beer? In many ways, beer at a ball game is one of those rites of passage that transcends generations. St. Louis, Missouri, native Adolphus Busch made his Budweiser brand beer available to baseball fans in the last quarter of the 19th century through his innovative use of refrigerated railcars to deliver the beverage. St. Louis Cardinals fans today who cheer on first baseman Mark McGwire in his quest for home run records often do so with a cup of Budweiser raised high. Back in the 1930s, their grandparents cheered on the Gashouse Gang Cardinals Dizzy Dean, Ducky Medwick, and Enos Slaughter much the same way.

But the sports fan of the 1930s would be astounded by the wide variety of food service available to the baseball, football, hockey, or basketball fan of the 21st century. Today, the fare for hungry baseball fans in San Diego or San Francisco includes sushi as well as hot dogs with relish. Phoenix Suns basketball fans can order nachos with melted jack cheese and jalapeño peppers instead of popcorn. Fans in line at the concession stands at Ralph Wilson Stadium in Buffalo may well order buffalo wings with bleu cheese dressing in place of peanuts, and fans at Baltimore's Oriole Park can have tarragon roasted chicken with their Cracker Jacks.

Concessions studies show that the old standards still prevail in the hearts and mouths of fans, but computerized food service equipment, including microwaves, warming trays, and flash-bake ovens, have made specialized food preparation for sporting and performance events far more efficient than in the past. New packaging techniques make prepared food delivery to skyboxes, luxury suites, and concession stands the rule rather than the exception nowadays. It's not just the same old hot dog anymore.

ABOVE: VENDORS AT TOKYO DOME IN JAPAN WORK THE CROWD. OPPOSITE: FANS OUTSIDE A SYDNEY, AUSTRALIA, BOX OFFICE EXAMINE THEIR TICKETS FOR THE 2000 OLYMPIC GAMES. TICKETS FOR THE SYDNEY OLYMPICS COULD ALSO BE BOUGHT BY PHONE AND ON THE INTERNET.

THE VIRTUAL FIELD HOUSE

Savvy facility managers are using the Internet to market their new arenas, auditoriums, performing arts centers, stadiums, and convention centers to cyberspace fans. It seems that there is hardly a public assembly facility that does not have its own Web site these days. Ticket and scheduling information, press releases, seating charts, staff directories, history of the site, press releases, and even driving directions

---

VIRTUAL TOURS

One of the public assembly facility manager's critical responsibilities is marketing his or her venue. Event Software's 3D Event Designer computer-aided design (CAD) application can help. This easy-to-learn-and-use software makes it simple to lay out three-dimensional floor plans for meetings, events, exhibits, etc. It is then possible to "walk through" the design and view it from any angle, which reveals potential hazards, sight obstructions, traffic patterns, lighting needs, and other factors that are hard to visualize. What's more, an optional viewer application and Internet compatibility make it possible to send the design directly to the client for review at his or her convenience.

INNOVATIVE THINKING

are becoming standard on-line offerings. Some sites, such as the Portland Rose Garden, home of the NBA's Trail Blazers, even offer a "Web cam" feature that lets Web crawlers "visit" the stadium and see what is happening at that moment.

The University of Nevada at Las Vegas (UNLV) Athletics home page not only offers both live and archived audio and video clips of Rebels games played on the university's home turf at Thomas & Mark Center; it also offers an on-line store where fans can buy team jerseys and other items. On-line shopping at PAF Web sites is becoming more and more common.

Many convention centers, such as Detroit's Cobo Conference/Exhibition Center, offer on-line registration via their Web sites for trade shows and other events. While many stadium and theater sites do not yet have the on-line capability to sell tickets directly, all offer a number to call for tickets, and many accept orders via e-mail.

Meanwhile, most of the nation's major ticket sellers have moved or are moving to cyberspace, and on-line ticket sales for sporting and entertainment events have been available through such channels for a few years now. An increasing number of ticket sellers are giving on-line ticket purchasers the option of printing out their own tickets using a personal computer.

Ticketmaster, a leader in the industry, launched its electronic ticket service in 1997. Through its partner, Ticketmaster Online–City Search, Ticketmaster.com maintains a database showing exactly who has purchased which ticket. In a new service scheduled for late 2000, the company will offer printable electronic tickets. The "E-ticket" will be encrypted with a bar code, which can be scanned at the game, concert, or show.

Unlike a ticket purchased at the box office, however, an encrypted on-line ticket can contain a wide variety of additional material. An electronic ticket might include a detailed map showing where the public assembly facility is located, a list of parking lots in the vicinity, and seating charts showing how to get to the seats purchased.

Montreal-based Admission Network, another ticket seller hoping to introduce on-line tickets for reproduction on personal computer printers, told the business press in early 2000 that all of its major clients, including the Molson Centre in Montreal, would soon be accepting electronic tickets. Through Admission Network, Canadian patrons now have Internet ticketing options for more than 1,900 sports, entertainment, and cultural events.

Another Internet company that is pioneering ticket selling on-line is Tickets.com. Founded in 1996, the firm was named the official ticketing services supplier to the 2002 Olympic Winter Games in Salt Lake City. In just four years, the Costa Mesa, California–based firm has signed Internet ticketing agreements involving more than 4,500 entertainment organizations. Through MyTickets, its personalization tool, Tickets.com offers ticket purchasers an electronic way to customize their sports and entertainment preferences. Tickets.com's computers keep track of purchases and e-mail customers when their favorite events are upcoming.

It's all in a day's work for the public assembly industry. But innovations in PAF operations and equipment don't just spring from thin air. They are the end result of years of work by inventors, tinkerers, engineers, and designers who have one goal in mind: To create the best possible experience for millions of fans and patrons worldwide.

And as the old saying goes, you ain't seen nothing yet.

OPERATIONS AND EQUIPMENT

SIX
CORPORATE PROFILES

PHOTO: © BETTMANN/CORBIS

OPERATORS & SPECIAL EQUIPMENT

DAKTRONICS INC.

DAKTRONICS INC., A LEADING MAKER OF STATE-OF-THE-ART SCOREBOARDS FOR SPORTS EVENTS WORLDWIDE, OFFERS A FULL SPECTRUM OF COMPUTER-BASED VIDEO AND DATA DISPLAYS.

Daktronics Inc. is known across the globe for its leading design and manufacture of fine computer-programmable display systems.

Founded in 1968 by two professors of electrical engineering, Daktronics—based in Brookings, South Dakota—specializes in providing products and services to sports facilities. The technology-driven company offers a full range of scoring and display products, from small digital clocks for locker rooms to some of the largest full-color video screens in the world.

The Daktronics track record includes extensive experience in presenting exciting visual communication at the most prestigious sports venues. The company has provided equipment and technical support for events from professional sports to major amateur athletic competitions to college games.

SAFECO FIELD, HOME TO THE SEATTLE MARINERS, USES AN INTEGRATED DAKTRONICS DISPLAY SYSTEM TO PROVIDE AN EVEN MORE ENTERTAINING AND INFORMATIVE EXPERIENCE FOR FANS. THE HUGE MAIN SCOREBOARD INCORPORATES BOTH LED VIDEO AND INCANDESCENT MATRIX DISPLAYS.

DISPLAYS FOR VIDEO, SCORES, & INFORMATION

With its unique capabilities, Daktronics is one of the few companies that can provide a truly integrated video, scoring, and information display system for a stadium or arena anywhere on the planet. The firm's manufacturing processes include component assembly, electronics assembly, printed circuit board fabrication, metal fabrication, welding, painting, and final assembly.

The 400,000 fans who attended the 2000 Indianapolis 500 can attest to the benefits of Daktronics products. The Indianapolis Motor Speedway chose Daktronics to provide 13 large ProStar® video screens and additional displays and scoreboards to help race fans enjoy events at the track even more.

At Cleveland's new football stadium, Browns fans watch highlights and replays on two of the largest video screens in the world, one behind each end zone. Each video display is approximately 30 feet high by 97 feet wide. The ProStar video displays are the most prominent components of the integrated scoring, information, and video display system, which was designed for the venue by Daktronics.

Major league baseball fans in Seattle receive more information and even more entertainment during a Mariners game, thanks to a variety of Daktronics displays. In addition to watching video replays on the large ProStar display behind center field, fans stay informed of player and team statistics, pitch speed and type, out-of-town game scores, and other data on Daktronics displays located throughout the ballpark. The displays are tied together and work together as an integrated system through the unique Daktronics networked control system.

THE DAKTRONICS PROSTAR® VIDEOPLUS DISPLAY AT SAFECO FIELD IN SEATTLE IS JUST ONE OF MANY IMPORTANT COMPONENTS THAT MAKE UP THE COMPANY'S INTEGRATED SCORING, VIDEO, AND INFORMATION DISPLAY SYSTEM.

State-of-the-Art Technologies for All Sports

Daktronics has the most complete line of scoreboards for all sports at all levels. Its products run the gamut from small portable models to some of the largest permanent scoreboard installations in the world. Daktronics has engineered scoring and display systems that keep track of the action at diverse sports competitions from archery to wrestling and every sport in between, including baseball, basketball, football, hockey, volleyball, golf, tennis, and even rodeos. World-class athletes check data on Daktronics systems at major international events such as the Olympic Games, the Pan American Games, and the Commonwealth Games. Student athletes and fans stay informed with Daktronics scoreboards during school games at thousands of gymnasiums and athletic fields worldwide.

While some manufacturers offer a single display technology, Daktronics makes available the full spectrum of state-of-the-art technologies, including light-emitting diode (LED), incandescent lamp/lens, and reflective displays for indoor and outdoor use. Daktronics offers a choice of character-based, line-oriented, and full-matrix systems. Each display technology has advantages for particular locations and situations. Part of the objective at Daktronics is helping clients determine the best display for a particular use.

THE CLEVELAND BROWNS STADIUM FEATURES TWO OF THE LARGEST VIDEO SCREENS IN THE WORLD. PROSTAR VIDEOPLUS DISPLAYS IN EACH END ZONE MEASURE APPROXIMATELY 30 FEET HIGH BY 97 FEET WIDE.

THANKS TO 13 DAKTRONICS PROSTAR DISPLAYS LOCATED AROUND THE TRACK, INDIANAPOLIS MOTOR SPEEDWAY FANS CAN ENJOY RACES EVEN MORE, BECAUSE THEY CAN SEE ALL THE ACTION ON THE ENTIRE TRACK.

Setting the Standards

Daktronics has maintained its leadership position in the industry by continuing to develop and refine products that meet and exceed client needs. In addition, the firm's use of modular design and construction keeps quality high, reduces costs to the customer, speeds delivery, and improves maintainability. Quality and reliability are further ensured with the use of microprocessor-based components, computer-aided design and drafting, solid-state electronics, and all-aluminum construction.

Daktronics assists its clients in every way possible to make sure they get the most from their scoring and display systems. A staff of professional graphic designers, animators, and video specialists is available. The firm's customer support service is among the best in the industry. At the Daktronics help desk, experienced technicians use the company's comprehensive database for immediate access to each customer's detailed record of equipment.

Installation supervision is available, provided by trained and experienced Daktronics technicians to ensure that each new system is installed and operating properly. Training seminars for customers' display operators are held throughout the year at locations across the nation. Daktronics also gives training seminars for customers' maintenance personnel on all aspects of equipment maintenance. In addition, Daktronics seeks out and trains only the most competent technicians to provide service for its products.

Daktronics is a longtime member of the International Association of Assembly Managers, the Stadium Managers Association, and the Information Display & Entertainment Association.

DAKTRONICS, INC.

ANHEUSER-BUSCH COMPANIES, INC.

AFTER GENERATIONS OF STEADY, INNOVATIVE GROWTH, ANHEUSER-BUSCH COMPANIES, INC., THE WORLD'S LARGEST BREWER AND ONE OF THE NATION'S LARGEST THEME PARK OPERATORS, CONTINUES TO PROSPER.

Every beer lover in America is familiar with Anheuser-Busch Companies, Inc. After all, the company, which has been brewing such high quality beers as Budweiser and Michelob for nearly a century and a half, has been at the top of the nation's brewing industry since 1957.

But not everyone is familiar with Anheuser-Busch's rich history, or with the fact that in addition to its impressive lineup of beers, the company also is involved in family entertainment, aluminum beverage container manufacturing and recycling, malt production, rice milling, real estate development, turf farming, creative services, metalized paper label printing, railroad car repair, and transportation services.

Like most major corporations, Anheuser-Busch sprang forth from modest beginnings. It began in 1860, when a successful St. Louis businessman, Eberhard Anheuser, financed a loan for a local Bavarian brewery that had been established in 1852. Anheuser eventually acquired the interests of the brewery's minority creditors and, in 1864, brought into the company his German immigrant son-in-law, Adolphus Busch, first as a salesman and eventually as a partner.

BASED IN ST. LOUIS, MISSOURI, ANHEUSER-BUSCH COMPANIES, INC., IS THE WORLD'S LARGEST BREWER, WITH SALES IN MORE THAN 80 COUNTRIES. THE COMPANY'S POPULAR PRODUCTS INCLUDE BEERS SUCH AS BUDWEISER, BUD LIGHT AND MICHELOB.

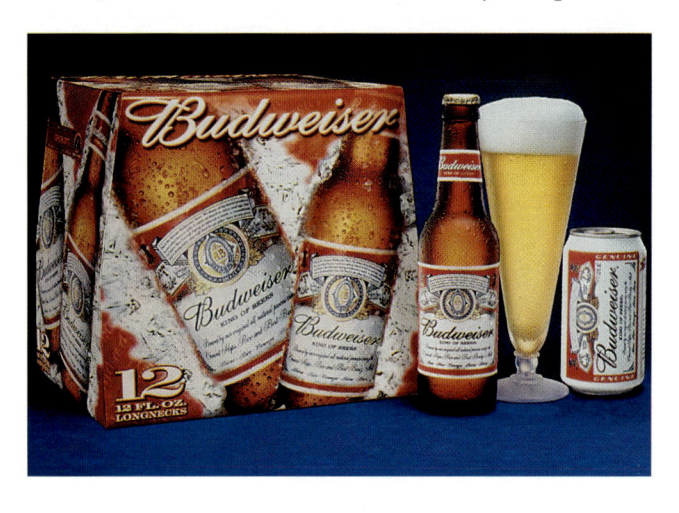

FAR-REACHING FOUNDATIONS FOR BUSINESS

It was Adolphus Busch who became the driving force that transformed the brewery into a giant in its industry nationally. To accomplish this, he launched the industry's first fleet of refrigerated freight cars, creating a network of railside icehouses to cool carloads of beer being shipped long distances. He also pioneered the use of pasteurization to ensure that his company's beer would remain fresh until it was consumed, wherever that might be.

In 1876, with his friend Carl Conrad, he developed Budweiser, the company's flagship beer, which continues to outsell all other beer brands in the world. Adolphus Busch assumed presidency of the firm in 1880. In 1896, he developed Michelob, Anheuser-Busch's preeminent superpremium beer.

Successive generations of the Busch family carried on and expanded the company's operations after Adolphus Busch's death, in 1913. His son, August A. Busch Sr. (1865-1934), guided the company through World War I, Prohibition, and the Great Depression—

ANHEUSER-BUSCH HAS BREWED AND SOLD BUDWEISER PREMIUM LAGER SINCE 1876. THE CRISP, DISTINCTIVE TASTE AND SMOOTH DRINKABILITY OF "THE KING OF BEERS" HAVE MADE BUDWEISER THE BEST-SELLING BEER IN THE WORLD.

three major successive upheavals that forced many other breweries to shut their doors. When Prohibition brought beer sales to a halt, he diversified the company, producing corn products, baker's yeast, ice cream, soft drinks, malt syrup, and commercial refrigeration units.

August Busch Sr.'s successor, his son Adolphus Busch III (1891-1946), made the company's baker's yeast operations the nation's leader, a position it held until the unit was sold, in 1988.

After Adolphus Busch III, the company was led by August A. Busch Jr. (1899-1989). He built eight regional breweries, increased annual beverage sales from three million to 34 million barrels, and began diversifying the company into family entertainment, real estate, can making, and transportation.

BUILDING ON SUCCESS

The next to assume leadership of Anheuser-Busch was August A. Busch III, currently chairman of the board and president of Anheuser-Busch Companies. Through his efforts, the company has opened three additional breweries, acquired another one, and introduced additional beer products to meet changing consumer preferences, including Bud Light, the nation's best-selling light beer; Michelob Light, the first superpremium light beer; O'Doul's, the top-selling, nonalcohol brew; Tequiza, the first malt beverage combining the tastes of lime and imported tequila; and "Doc" Otis', a slightly sweet-flavored "malternative" malt beverage, made with real lemon juice and just the right amount of tartness, appealing to consumers looking for alternatives to beers, mixed drinks, wines, and wine coolers. In addition, under August Busch III, the company has expanded its entertainment business; launched its largest-ever brewery expansions; and diversified into international brewing, container recovery, metalized label printing, and creative services.

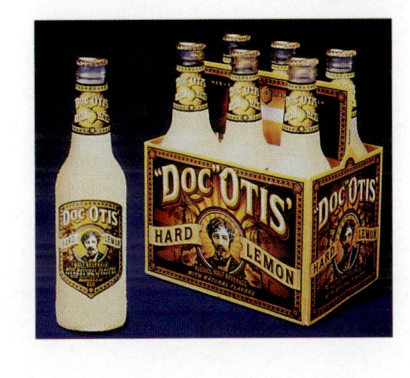

BUSCH ENTERTAINMENT CORPORATION, ANHEUSER-BUSCH'S FAMILY ENTERTAINMENT SUBSIDIARY, IS ONE OF THE LEADING THEME PARK OPERATORS IN THE UNITED STATES. SHOWN HERE IS BUSCH GARDENS TAMPA BAY, THE FIRST ANHEUSER-BUSCH THEME PARK, A 335-ACRE, AFRICAN-THEMED FAMILY ADVENTURE PARK THAT FEATURES NATURALISTIC ANIMAL ATTRACTIONS, ENTERTAINMENT, AND THRILLING RIDES. © BUSCH ENTERTAINMENT CORPORATION.

Today Anheuser-Busch stands as the world's largest brewer. It also is one of the nation's largest adventure and theme park operators, with such well-known parks as Busch Gardens in Tampa, Florida, and Williamsburg, Virginia; and SeaWorld in Orlando, Florida, San Diego, California, San Antonio, Texas, and Cleveland, Ohio. The company is one of the largest U.S. manufacturers of aluminum beverage containers; the world's largest recycler of such containers; and the manufacturer of more than 15 billion metalized labels annually for its own operations and for other customers.

But despite its evolution into a major conglomerate, Anheuser-Busch continues the unwavering commitment to high quality that was at the heart of the company's operations when it started, in 1852.

Moreover, the innovative spirit that Adolphus Busch exhibited more than 100 years ago in making Budweiser the first national beer remains the primary reason behind Anheuser-Busch's current success and its formula for continued greatness.

Unquestionably, Adolphus Busch, were he alive today, would be proud of what his enterprise has wrought.

ANHEUSER-BUSCH'S NEWEST PRODUCT, "DOC" OTIS', IS A SLIGHTLY SWEET-FLAVORED "MALTERNATIVE" MALT BEVERAGE MADE WITH REAL LEMON JUICE AND JUST THE RIGHT AMOUNT OF TARTNESS. ON THE BACK LABEL OF EACH "DOC" OTIS' BOTTLE IS ONE OF SIX NARRATIVES ABOUT THE LEGENDARY EXPLOITS OF JEBEDIAH "DOC" OTIS, A FICTIONAL EXPLORER AND A BREWER OF HARD LEMON-FLAVORED BEVERAGES IN THE WILD WEST OF THE 1800s.

CLARIN
A DIVISION OF GREENWICH INDUSTRIES, L.P.

IN 2000, CLARIN CELEBRATES 75 YEARS OF LEADERSHIP IN PORTABLE SEATING WITH A PRODUCT LINE BASED ON ITS ORIGINAL X-FRAME STEEL FOLDING CHAIR DESIGN—A FAVORITE OF EVENT FACILITIES THROUGHOUT THE COUNTRY.

TO ACHIEVE SEATING FLEXIBILITY, THE MANDALAY BAY EVENT CENTER IN LAS VEGAS, NEVADA, PURCHASED 2,400 CLARIN FOLDING CHAIRS THAT FEATURE A UNIQUE PAINT COLOR AND CUSTOM UPHOLSTERY.

In 1925 Werner Clarin started a company to make steel folding chairs of his own design. His new chair—the first all-steel folding chair in the United States—was a huge hit. Since then, people have screamed for Sinatra and Sting, watched Bob Cousy or Michael Jordan, nominated candidates for the presidency, or spurred social reform while sitting on Clarin chairs in major arenas, convention centers, stadiums, and auditoriums throughout the nation.

Today, Clarin, a division of Greenwich Industries, L.P., in Lake Bluff, Illinois, remains the chairmaker of choice for such facilities. Clarin attributes this popularity to its chairs' quality—which begins with the X-style steel frame of double tube-and-channel construction invented by the founder. The chair remains intact even when jumped on, kicked, knocked over, and continually subjected to being set up and taken down. The flexible design distributes weight evenly to all four chair legs without rocking or tilting. When unoccupied, the chair reverts to its original shape. The style folds narrowly to maximize storage space.

Through the years, chair features have been added, appealing to today's facility owners who realize that the seating they select can have an impact on their facility's reputation and economic performance. Attractive, comfortable chairs with accessories such as chair arms and cup holders can enhance patrons' overall experiences at an event. The proper selection also can increase the seating capacity of a facility. Clarin offers the options of fold-up seats, erect or standard pitch seat backs, various seat-padding thicknesses, and easy-to-use ganging devices for handling a group of chairs as a unit.

Since a modern event facility is designed as a showplace, its furnishings must enhance its image. In response, Clarin offers a rainbow of color choices and a wide variety of upholstery fabrics to complement decor. Chair coverings also can be silk-screened, embroidered, or embossed with the name of a facility or its major tenant.

Clarin recognizes that its success during the past 75 years is due to the confidence each of its valued customers has shown in its ability to provide products and services to fit specific needs. Clarin is committed to continuing to provide innovative seating products to meet all its customers' future needs as well.

AT THE FAMILY ARENA IN ST. LOUIS/ST. CHARLES, MISSOURI, 2,100 CUSHIONED CLARIN PORTABLE CHAIRS PROVIDE MANY SEATING OPTIONS FOR MEETINGS AND EVENTS.

TICKETS.COM

TICKETS.COM ENABLES SPORTS, CULTURAL, AND ENTERTAINMENT ORGANIZATIONS BY OFFERING A VARIETY OF CUTTING-EDGE TICKETING SOLUTIONS AND SERVICES.

ONE OF TICKETS.COM'S VENUES IS THE BALLPARK IN ARLINGTON, HOME OF THE TEXAS RANGERS BASEBALL TEAM.

Tickets.com (Nasdaq: TIXX) is a leading on-line provider of sports and entertainment tickets, event information, and software solutions for event venues. Tickets.com sells tickets through the Internet, software licensees, retail outlets, call centers, and interactive voice response systems. At the Tickets.com Web site (www.tickets.com), consumers can obtain information on thousands of events and entertainment organizations, purchase tickets, and shop for related products and services.

Tickets.com's automated ticketing solutions are used by more than 4,500 entertainment organizations, such as leading performing arts centers, professional sports organizations, and various stadiums and arenas in the United States, Canada, Europe, Australia, and Latin America.

THE EMERSON MAJESTIC THEATRE, A 1903 LANDMARK, IS A PERFORMING ARTS CENTER LOCATED IN THE HEART OF THE HISTORIC THEATER DISTRICT OF BOSTON, MASSACHUSETTS.

Tickets.com's core objective is to *enable* entertainment organizations. To this end, Tickets.com facilitates the sale of tickets by providing:

- cutting-edge software solutions,
- flexible distribution alternatives,
- electronic gateways that allow for brand or private-label customer experiences, and
- a proactive ticket-selling approach driven by cooperation with customer venues to maximize ticket sales.

The result is a company committed to leveraging its technology to fundamentally change the ticketing industry by enabling businesses and empowering consumers.

Tickets.com offers a unique portfolio of systems and services that opens up more opportunities for ticketing and marketing than ever before.

TICKETS.COM'S OUTSTANDING MARKETING PRESENCE

- 2002 Olympic Winter Games, Salt Lake
- American Repertory Theatre
- Buffalo Sabres
- Carrier Dome
- Chicago Cubs
- Cornell University
- Dallas Stars
- Edmonton Oilers
- Emerson Majestic Theatre
- Ericsson Open
- Jacksonville Jaguars
- Lincoln Center
- Lowe's Motor Speedway
- Major League Baseball
- National Air and Space Museum
- National Museum of Natural History
- New York Philharmonic
- Ruth Eckerd Hall
- San Francisco Giants
- Texas Rangers
- UNLV

WHITE WAY SIGN COMPANY

WHITE WAY SIGN COMPANY OF CHICAGO IS RESPECTED BY SATISFIED CUSTOMERS WORLDWIDE FOR ITS BUSINESS IDENTIFICATION AND CUSTOM-MADE SIGNAGE, CREATED WITH QUALITY DESIGN, FABRICATION, AND SERVICE.

CHICAGO'S ORIENTAL THEATRE IS JUST ONE EXAMPLE OF WHITE WAY SIGN COMPANY'S 80-PLUS YEARS OF EXPERIENCE AND EXCELLENCE IN THE BUSINESS IDENTIFICATION AND CUSTOM-DESIGNED SIGNAGE INDUSTRY.

If one technology were to be chosen to characterize industrialized society in the 21st century, it might be communications. From cable television and cell phones to satellite uplinks and the Internet, daily life today is profoundly influenced by increasingly sophisticated systems for conveying every sort of information.

One communication discipline—the making of commercial and public signs—combines literally dazzling use of emergent technology and the same deep urges that have inspired imagery since history's first artists painted on cave walls. Today's electronic signage ranks among the most imaginative and appealing visual elements in public life, and one of the best-known makers of these is White Way Sign Company of Chicago.

Founded by Thomas F. Flannery Sr. in 1916, the firm has become a global leader in custom-designed signs for the commercial, casino, and sports markets. White Way's immense portfolio of installations includes signs for just about every imaginable venue and setting, from the Oriental Theatre to Lambeau Field, from Wrigley Field to Staples Center, from Madison Square Garden to the brand new Nationwide Arena.

From inception, the company has pursued its business goals with a strong emphasis on good taste rather than mere glitter. Says the president of White Way Sign, Robert B. Flannery Jr., "As a business carefully run by the same family for four generations, we understand that our most prized possession is our reputation. A sign is the most visible calling card for the company or structure it represents and must complement its environment while performing successful identification. Our success comes directly from the dignity and image our product represents to the public."

White Way Sign's adaptation of diverse technology includes the computer-controlled incandescent lamp matrix, full-color LED displays, reader boards, wedge-based lamp technology, flexible-face displays, and the installation of video displays. Traditional methods also can make a distinguished display, and White Way designers use them when appropriate. In cities worldwide, the company's installations—from moderate to monumental—combine imaginative communication and persuasive design. Several elegant and memorable White Way marquees and signs have been rendered by painter Robert Cottingham and were recently exhibited at the Smithsonian's National Museum of American Art.

Whether at gleaming new ballparks and stadiums or at prestigious commercial venues, the art and technology of White Way Sign are certain to inform and illuminate America's public life for a long time to come.

AT STAPLES CENTER, WHEN THE LOS ANGELES LAKERS, CLIPPERS, AND KINGS WANT TO LET THEIR FANS KNOW THE SCORE, THEY TURN TO WHITE WAY.

WHITE WAY SIGN COMPANY

SYLVAN INDUSTRIES INC.

A PROVIDER OF CUSTOM-MADE PANELS FOR PUBLIC FACILITIES, SYLVAN INDUSTRIES INC. IS A LEADER IN ITS FIELD, OFFERING INNOVATIVE, AWARD-WINNING PRODUCTS AND IMPORTANT SOLUTIONS TO CLIENTS AROUND THE WORLD.

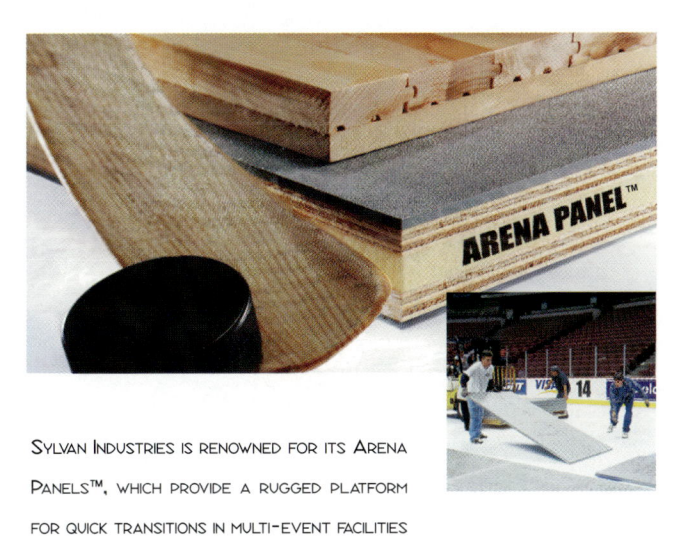

SYLVAN INDUSTRIES IS RENOWNED FOR ITS ARENA PANELS™, WHICH PROVIDE A RUGGED PLATFORM FOR QUICK TRANSITIONS IN MULTI-EVENT FACILITIES AND ICE RINKS. ARENA PANELS ARE FABRICATED TO SPECIFIED DESIGNS AND SIZES, THUS ENABLING OPTIMUM EFFICIENCY AND PERFORMANCE AT EACH FACILITY.

www.sylvan-products.com/arenas

Toughness...On Top of Everything Else

In less than a decade, Sylvan Industries Inc. has already become an industry leader. Founded in 1990 by W. Scott Wilson and A. Craig Digman, this Portland, Oregon–based company provides custom-made panels for such public facilities as ice arenas, stadiums, airports, universities, hotels, casinos, parking garages, and more.

For clients ranging from architect to builder, and from operations manager to the public itself, Sylvan provides construction products and Arena Panels™ for a wide variety of facilities and requirements. Along with its custom-made products, Sylvan is well known for its uncompromising service and its ability to respond to a wide range of challenges.

"Our relationship with our clients is solution-based rather than product-based," says Wilson. "And though this difference is seemingly subtle, the results for our customers are supremely significant. Since all our products are made to order, inventory issues are never an ulterior influence in our recommendations. This is the key to our success. Our goal to find the best solution for every challenge has proven to be a 'win-win' for both our clients and ourselves."

This proactive philosophy has won Sylvan numerous major assignments, including projects for Disneyland and Arrowhead Pond in Anaheim, America West Arena in Phoenix, Key Arena in Seattle, Pepsi Center in Denver, Staples Center in Los Angeles, and the Vityaz Ice Palace in Moscow, Russia. It has also brought Sylvan a number of accolades. Two awards, the AGC Build America Merit Award and the "Extraordinary Results in Concrete," were given to projects that featured Sylvan's DURA-POUR® concrete-form panels, which provide a stunning marblelike finish to columns and walls. Sylvan is also world renowned for its Arena Panel, which features stellar durability, affordable pricing, convenient reversibility, and slip-resistance, all of which make it "the ice-cover panel" for savvy operations managers in the arena events industry. In addition, an Airshow Innovation Award was given to Sylvan for its provision of lightweight tarmac panels used under the wheels of aircraft for international flight teams.

Sylvan plans to continue to raise the level of expectation for the performance of panels, while also striving to keep costs at an affordable level. "In the end, our mission is to produce extraordinary performance from exacting combinations of ordinary materials, because this allows each facility to keep costs in line with their budgets, while also getting extended life out of our products," says Wilson. However, Sylvan's growth lies in more than innovative manufacturing. Wilson explains, "When we strive to do the right thing every day, we not only enrich our relationships with our clients, business partners, and employees, but we also enable Sylvan to establish a business standard that we can be proud of for life."

SCOTT WILSON, FAR LEFT, AND CRAIG DIGMAN FOUNDED SYLVAN IN 1990 WITH A GOAL OF "BEING SOLUTIONS PROVIDERS, NOT JUST PRODUCT PEDDLERS."

AMERICAN SEATING COMPANY

AN INNOVATOR AND MANUFACTURER OF ARENA, STADIUM, AUDITORIUM, TRANSPORTATION, AND OFFICE PRODUCTS,

AMERICAN SEATING COMPANY SERVES PRESTIGIOUS VENUES NATIONWIDE.

AMERICAN SEATING COMPANY PROVIDED SEATING FOR ENRON FIELD, HOME OF THE HOUSTON ASTROS, IN HOUSTON, TEXAS, WHICH OPENED IN MARCH 2000 AND SEATS 42,000 FANS. © AMERICAN SEATING COMPANY

Millions of people are acquainted with the American Seating Company through its products, which furnish facilities ranging from New York City to Los Angeles.

American Seating is a leading manufacturer of auditorium seating, transportation seating, and contract office furniture. The firm was founded in 1886 as the Grand Rapids Furniture Company. The fledgling business employed 50 people to make the firm's primary product—a combination desk for students that joined a desktop and book box with a seat and back.

Today, American Seating has three divisions, serving three distinct markets—transportation products, office products, and architectural products. The architectural products group designs public seating for stadiums, arenas, auditoriums, and classrooms. Its products can be found in many of the nation's most prestigious sports arenas, including Comerica Park in Detroit, Yankee Stadium in New York City, Wrigley Field in Chicago, Enron Field in Houston, Pacific Bell Park in San Francisco, and Cleveland Browns Stadium, as well as other well-known public venues, such as Radio City Music Hall in New York City, the Crystal Cathedral in Garden Grove, California, and Benaroya Hall in Seattle.

American Seating introduced the first tilt-back opera chair, in 1893, and since then, the company has continued to lead the seating industry in innovative product design. Thanks to American Seating's three-quarter safety-fold stadium seat, sports fans can easily sit down on a folding seat while holding food and beverages. American Seating also led the industry in developing molded plastic seats, made necessary in 1958 when the trees used to make major league stadium seats, traditionally of steam-bent elm, were depleted by Dutch Elm disease. American Seating currently employs more than 800 people at its main facility in Grand Rapids, Michigan, and also has manufacturing operations in Winchester, Tennessee, and Orillia, Ontario, Canada.

The American Seating management team purchased the company in 1987. "Since that time, we have experienced steady growth and have made a major commitment to building our company in the city of Grand Rapids," says Edward Clark, president and CEO.

American Seating strongly believes that the key to its success now and in the future is its employees. "We have a great team of people here and relationships that are based on trust," Clark says. "Because of their efforts, we have become a thriving, revitalized company. In the coming years, we look forward to continued success while maintaining our tradition of excellence and industry leadership."

★AmericanSeating

AMERICAN SEATING PRODUCTS FILL THE 91,000-SQUARE-FOOT CRYSTAL CATHEDRAL, IN GARDEN GROVE, CALIFORNIA, WHICH HAS SEATING FOR 2,900. © AMERICAN SEATING COMPANY

R.I.C. CORP.

SOFTWARE COMPANY R.I.C. CORP. MAKES CONCENTRICS FACILITY-MANAGEMENT SOFTWARE, A FLEXIBLE SYSTEM USED SUCCESSFULLY BY FACILITIES WORLDWIDE, LARGE AND SMALL, TO HANDLE EVENTS OF ALL KINDS.

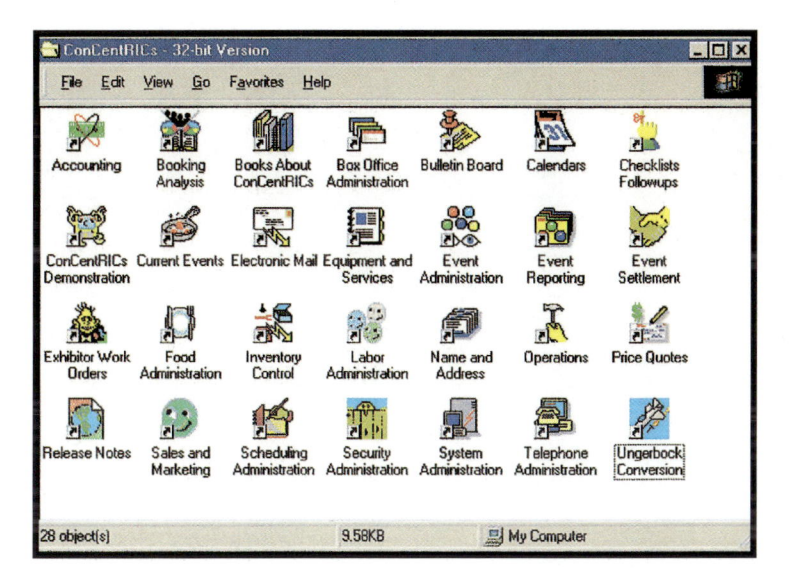

THE COMPREHENSIVE FACILITY-MANAGEMENT CONCENTRICS SOFTWARE, BY R.I.C. CORP., OFFERS MANY MODULES FOR HANDLING EVENT PROCESSES. ITS TWO BASIC, REQUIRED MODULES ARE SYSTEM ADMINISTRATION AND SCHEDULING ADMINISTRATION.

Since its inception in 1982, the mission of R.I.C. Corp., based in Fort Wayne, Indiana, has been to produce the ultimate in software systems that help manage facilities. Its product ConCentRICs, which is widely known throughout the industry, is thought to be the most comprehensive facility-management software available and is used in more than 40 facilities worldwide.

R.I.C. president and cofounder, Rick Kriscka, and financial officer and cofounder, Joan Tracey, are the architects of the original prototype of ConCentRICs. "R.I.C. interviewed facility personnel who actually book and manage events, including salespeople, event managers, accountants, and others," says Kriscka. "Their processes and procedures are mirrored in the design of ConCentRICs." In addition, software enhancements and priorities are determined by the user community.

ConCentRICs, which is short for "Convention Center Reporting Information and Control System," is not short on applications and flexibility. The software has been used successfully by conference and convention centers, arenas, stadiums, auditoriums, performing arts theaters, banquet halls, resorts, hotels, and universities.

ConCentRICs provides a separate module for each department in a facility, to eliminate the paperwork involved in various functions and provide ease of use and security. Facility staff members have access only to the options they need to perform their jobs. All modules are fully integrated, so information is entered just once. The system can handle all steps of facility management from initial contact with clients through to final billing, as well as management of inventory, staff, and World Wide Web sites. It also can produce floor plans automatically for easier event setup. Updated profit-and-loss statements can be accessed at any moment, for an event or for a specified period of time.

The modular design of the ConCentRICs system also means a facility can begin with the applications that best meet its needs and budget, and phase in other applications later. The scalable software works as well for a smaller operation with just one computer as for a large enterprise with networked workstations in different geographic locations.

A facility becomes a voting member of the nonprofit International Association of ConCentRICs Users (IACU) once it has purchased the software. Members can propose changes to the software and, if approved, the revisions are made and posted on the IACU link of the R.I.C. Web site (www.riccorp.com), to be downloaded free of charge by members.

RICK KRISCKA, PRESIDENT, AND JOAN TRACEY, FINANCIAL OFFICER, ARE COFOUNDERS OF R.I.C. CORP., HEADQUARTERED IN FORT WAYNE, INDIANA.

TICKETMASTER

TICKETMASTER CONTINUES TO CREATE THE FUTURE, MAKING ENTERTAINMENT TICKETS CONVENIENTLY AVAILABLE FOR PURCHASE AT RETAIL TICKET CENTERS, BY TELEPHONE, AND SOON, WITH A PERSONAL COMPUTER PRINTER.

Ticketmaster is one of the most viable and hands-on customer service success stories of the 20th century. Founded in 1976 in Arizona by two college students, its proactive and innovative approach in meeting the demands of a changing marketplace has revolutionized both the ticketing and customer service industry. By providing service, convenience, access, and value to its clients and the ticket-buying public, Ticketmaster has become the world's leading ticket distribution service.

Ticketmaster remains devoted to the needs of its clients through its development of computer software and hardware systems. The company is constantly striving to make the purchasing of tickets for entertainment events more convenient and accessible. In 1997, Ticketmaster launched its World Wide Web site (www.ticketmaster.com), giving thousands of consumers the ability to purchase their event tickets on-line and making Ticketmaster the world's number one on-line ticketing company.

TERRY BARNES, CHAIRMAN AND CEO OF TICKETMASTER GROUP, INC., JOINED TICKETMASTER MORE THAN 17 YEARS AGO AND NOW HEADS THE COMPANY, WHICH HAS BECOME THE WORLD'S LEADING TICKETING SERVICE, WITH ANNUAL SALES OF MORE THAN $3 BILLION.
© ANNAMARIA DISANTO

AS TICKETMASTER GROUP, INC., PRESIDENT AND CHIEF OPERATING OFFICER, LARRY JACOBSON OVERSEES THE DAY-TO-DAY OPERATIONS OF TICKETMASTER AND ITS AFFILIATED COMPANIES. ADDITIONALLY, JACOBSON IS RESPONSIBLE FOR THE DEVELOPMENT OF STRATEGIC ALLIANCES BETWEEN TICKETMASTER AND THE USA NETWORK FAMILY OF COMPANIES.

Currently, through its partnership with Ticketmaster Online–CitySearch, Inc., Ticketmaster is beta testing printable electronic "E-tickets." The service enables the consumer to select a desired event, purchase a ticket for the event on-line via ticketmaster.com and print the ticket using an office or home printer. The E-ticket contains a bar code and is scanned for admission to the event like a traditional ticket. This new and convenient method of ticketing is expected to be rolled out throughout the United States in late 2000. In response to the security and marketing needs of its clients, Ticketmaster has developed a state-of-the-art, bar code inventory control system that provides consumers with instant tickets and simultaneously monitors customer habits and buying patterns.

Guided by Ticketmaster chairman and CEO, Terry Barnes, and president and COO, Larry Jacobson, Ticketmaster sells more than 75 million event tickets for its more than 5,000 clients in Argentina, Australia, Canada, Chile, Ireland, Latin America, the United Kingdom, and the United States. Annual ticket sales for Ticketmaster, which is now owned by parent company USA Networks, Inc., are more than $3 billion.

Customers of Ticketmaster have convenient access to tickets for more than 350,000 events per year through Ticketmaster's 3,400-plus retail ticket center outlets, its 16 telephone call centers worldwide, and its Web site www.ticketmaster.com.

101

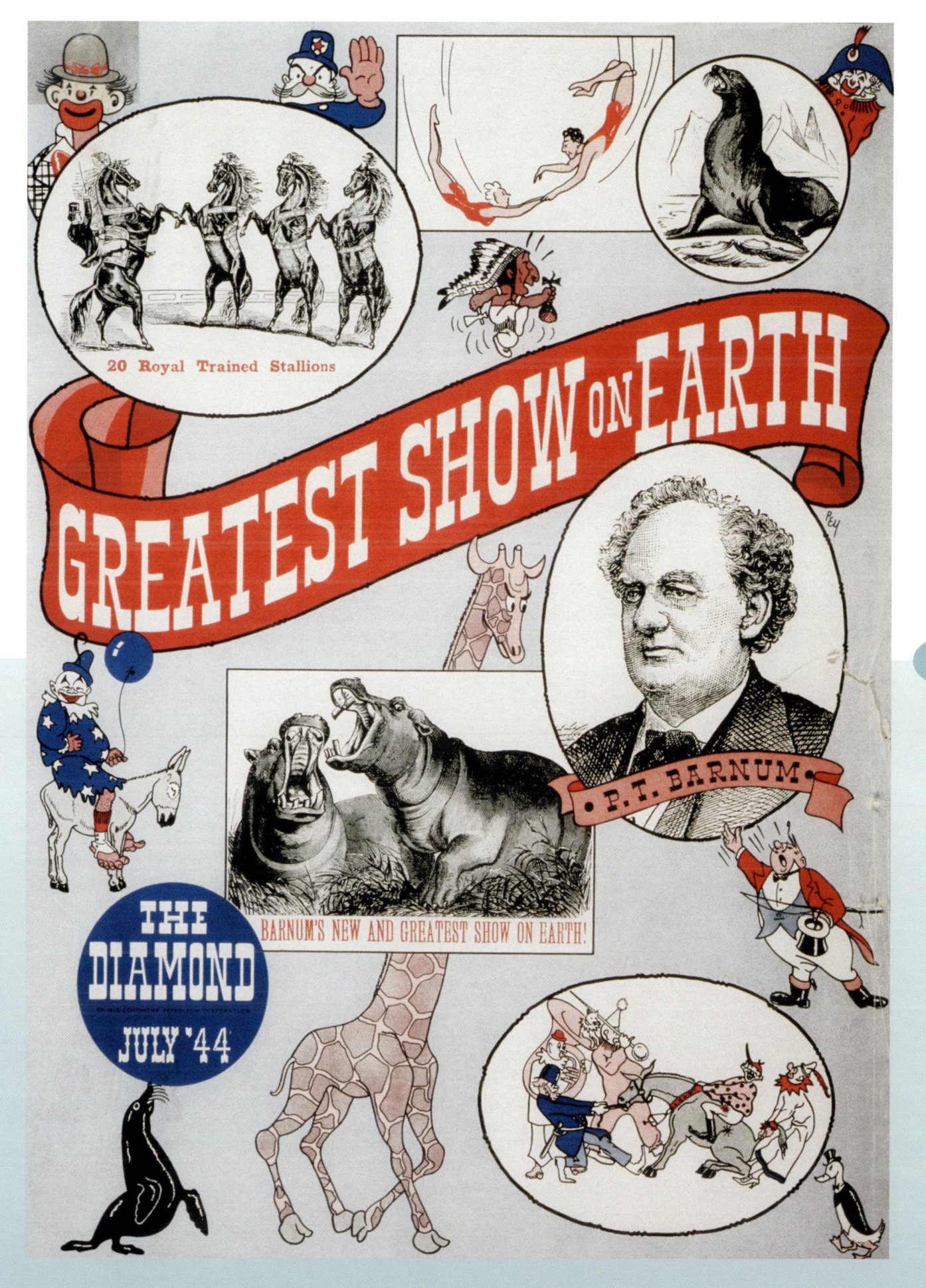

SEVEN
COMING ATTRACTIONS: THE FUTURE OF THE PUBLIC FACILITIES INDUSTRY

THE WORLD OF PUBLIC ASSEMBLY FACILITIES IS NOT STATIC. EVER SINCE PUBLIC ASSEMBLY FACILITIES AND MODERN ENTERTAINMENT VENUES BEGAN TO MAKE THEIR MARK WITH mass audiences in the 19th century, facility managers and their colleagues in the convention and tourism/hospitality businesses have pioneered innovations in crowd management, ticket sales, concessions, and maintenance and operations. These new ideas have made events more convenient, affordable, and safe for billions of people around the globe. That record of innovation is likely to continue well into the 21st century.

Public assembly facility managers and communities around the world will come up with new and cost-effective ways to finance stadiums, performing arts centers, amphitheaters, convention centers, and other such facilities. Marketing managers will devise groundbreaking ways to create brand recognition for public assembly facilities in the years to come. Engineers and equipment manufacturers will design and install machinery and operating technologies that will make the Zamboni and AstroTurf seem primitive by comparison. Concessions managers will make eating out at the stadium, amphitheater, or other public assembly facility equivalent to dining in a fine restaurant.

PRIVATIZING THE PUBLIC ASSEMBLY FACILITY

Perhaps the hottest trend in financing public assembly facilities at the dawn of the new millennium is privatization. For years, public assembly facilities were just that: *public* assembly facilities. But increasingly, public assembly facilities have become public-private assembly facilities, or even all-private assembly facilities.

More and more public assembly facilities are managed by private management companies. And a growing number of these private management companies are publicly traded.

The trend got its start in the late 1980s and early 1990s when many major-league sports franchises crossed over into ownership of the stadiums, arenas, and ballparks where their teams played. The Tribune Company, owner of

ABOVE, LEFT TO RIGHT: LUXURY SUITES SUCH AS THIS ONE AT THE CROWN COLISEUM IN FAYETTEVILLE, NORTH CAROLINA, ARE BECOMING COMMON IN NEW ARENAS AND STADIUMS. • THE BEST LOCKER ROOM RESTAURANT, ON THE EVENT LEVEL AT INDIANAPOLIS'S CONSECO FIELDHOUSE, CAN BE USED FOR PRIVATE PARTIES. • MILWAUKEE'S MIDWEST EXPRESS CENTER BALLROOM IS EQUIPPED LIKE A CONCERT HALL FOR CORPORATE THEATER PRESENTATIONS. OPPOSITE: THE HOME COURT TEAM STORE AT CONSECO FIELDHOUSE FEATURES INDIANA PACERS AND OTHER LOCAL-TEAM MERCHANDISE.

103

major league baseball's Chicago Cubs, also owns venerable Wrigley Field on Chicago's north side. Microsoft cofounder Paul Allen is a majority owner of both the NBA's Portland Trail Blazers and the team's home court, the Rose Garden in Portland. Daniel Snyder, the youthful owner of the National Football League's Washington Redskins, is also the owner of Jack Kent Cooke Stadium.

Private owners do exactly what the name implies. They own the stadium or public assembly facility in which the team plays. The private owner often arranges financing for the construction of the facility, although very few private owners have the wherewithal to finance the $300 million to $500 million that is needed to build a new facility today. The private owners might finance the lion's share of new construction, but public agencies are usually called upon to finance infrastructure construction, highway access, and parking structures. The municipality will often agree to this because a professional sports franchise is typically a matter of great community pride. The public financing can come in the form of tax increment financing districts, local option taxes, and hotel, beverage, and entertainment taxes.

A variation on the theme of private ownership occurs when the team that is a tenant of the facility holds a long-term lease on the facility. Lease tenants are like owners in that they typically have an interest in making substantial improvements to the facility. But unlike owners, lease tenants have the option of going elsewhere to play once the lease is up, or if attendance doesn't hit contractually agreed-upon targets. The clamor for new stadiums in communities such as Minneapolis–St. Paul and San Antonio frequently comes from lease tenants who are unhappy with their current lease.

The third and most rapidly growing segment of private management is what industry observers call "contracted management services." Dozens of companies nationwide contract with public assembly facility owners to manage those facilities for an annual fee.

In recent years, consolidation has been the name of the game in the facility management business. By far the largest facility management firm in the United States is SMG, based in Philadelphia. Founded in 1988, SMG has become a world leader in the growing field of management of public assembly facilities. In early 2000, the company operated 64 facilities around the world. SMG has facility management contracts for 23 convention centers, nine theaters, eight professional sports stadiums, and food and beverage operations at two aquariums.

Approximately 92 percent of the publicly owned exhibition space in the United States that is operated by private companies is managed by SMG. The company manages more than 5.9 million square feet of exhibition space at the 23 convention centers it has under contract. The arenas and convention centers under management, which range from Norway's Oslo Spektrum to the Long Beach Arena to the Tampa Ice Palace, have a total capacity of almost 280,000 seats.

SMG manages and provides services to theaters, for a total capacity of 29,900 seats. Its eight stadiums include Three Rivers Stadium in Pittsburgh, the Louisiana Superdome in New Orleans, Soldier Field in Chicago, Mile High Stadium in Denver, and ALLTEL Stadium in Jacksonville. SMG-managed stadiums play host to six National Football League (NFL) teams and more than 350

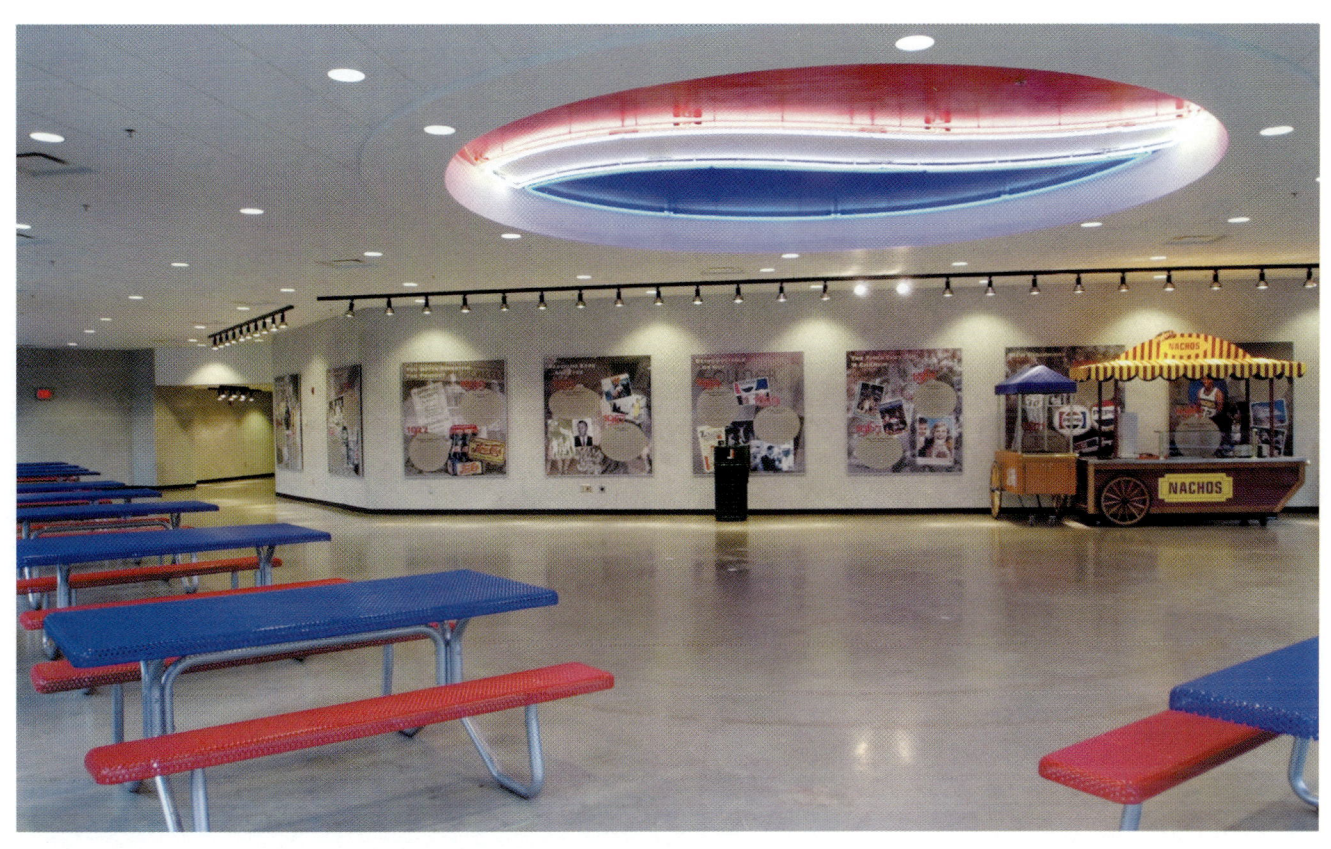

ABOVE: CONSECO FIELDHOUSE'S SLEEK PEPSI SQUARE IS PERFECT FOR A PREGAME PICNIC.
OPPOSITE: THIS RENDERING OF MILWAUKEE'S MILLER PARK SHOWS THE UNION OF HIGH TECHNOLOGY AND NOSTALGIC BALLPARK DESIGN DESIRED BY MANY COMMUNITIES IN THE NEW MILLENNIUM.

sporting events, family shows, concerts, conventions, and trade shows each year.

SMG recently purchased another industry leader, Leisure Management International (LMI). LMI's stable of management contracts includes the El Paso Convention Center, the ALLTEL Arena in Little Rock, the Palm Springs Convention Center, the Nashville Arena, Pro Player Stadium in Miami, and some two dozen others.

SMG is jointly owned by the Hyatt Hotel chain and ARAMARK Corporation, one of the world's largest service companies. ARAMARK also recently acquired substantially all of the food and beverage concessions and venue management businesses of Ogden Corporation, which has a strong presence in the nation's energy, entertainment, and aviation sectors. Ogden's clients include Wrigley Field in Chicago, the STAPLES Center in Los Angeles, the Pepsi Center in Denver, Veterans Stadium in Philadelphia, and the MCI Center in Washington, D.C.

Regional management firms are also active in the public assembly facility field. Compass Facility Management, specializing in smaller-market public facilities, manages arenas, theaters, amphitheaters, and convention centers in North Dakota, Iowa, and Minnesota. Another player, Global Spectrum, provides management and consulting services to facilities in various parts of the United States, including the Jerome Schottenstein Center at Ohio State University, the Colorado Springs World Arena, the Thomas J. White Stadium in Port St. Lucie, Florida, and about a dozen others. In partnership with the Asia-based Pico Group, Global Spectrum's GSA Asia, Ltd., serves clients in China, Thailand, and Malaysia.

Contracted management service firms usually serve city-, county-, and university-owned facilities. They charge a base fee and typically build in benchmark incentives that can increase the annual fee substantially. Benchmark incentive fees can be attached to a number of different factors, including number of events managed, attendance, and gross revenue. Public assembly facility owners can also write the contracts to require penalties if minimum goals aren't met, and most contracts between public assembly facilities and contracted

THE FUTURE OF THE PUBLIC FACILITIES INDUSTRY

SEVEN

COMING ATTRACTIONS

LEFT: THE MIDWEST WIRELESS CIVIC CENTER IN MANKATO, MINNESOTA, IS AMONG AN INCREASING NUMBER OF MEETING, SPORTS, AND ENTERTAINMENT FACILITIES THAT CONTRACT FOR MANAGEMENT SERVICES. OPPOSITE: JAPAN'S SAITAMA SUPER ARENA INCORPORATES ENERGY-EFFICIENT DESIGN BY UTILIZING LARGE AMOUNTS OF GLASS TO LET IN NATURAL LIGHT. THE CURVED ROOF IS 66 METERS ABOVE GRADE.

management service firms being written today typically require the private management firm to make some kind of up-front financial investment in the facility.

Steve Peters, founder and president of Compass Facility Management, noted recently that performance-driven contracts are becoming the rule, rather than the exception, in contracted service management. Performance-driven contracts provide incentives to both sides. The public assembly facility can limit its expense exposure, and the management firm can make more money than on a fixed contract. But the private-public management of public assembly facilities must live with tax implications and financial restrictions that management firms in other sectors of the economy might find unworkable.

According to Peters, the Tax Reform Act of 1986 imposed significant restrictions on management contracts for facilities financed all or in part by tax-exempt bonds, an extremely common financing venue from the 1960s to the 1990s. Under terms of the 1986 act, management firms cannot exceed base fees. Public assembly facility owners may sign a five-year contract with a private management firm, but the law allows the public assembly facility to exit the contract after three years. Finally, the private management firm cannot participate in profit sharing from the public assembly facility.

"Despite these challenges," Peters wrote, "private management continues to grow. More owners own. More tenants lease. And more local governments and universities turn to private management companies."

> ### SUPERSMART CONSTRUCTION
>
> Japan's new Saitama Super Arena has been dubbed the world's first "smart arena." Located in a north Tokyo suburb, Saitama's "moving block" (MB) construction design allows it to convert from an intimate concert venue to a full-fledged stadium in less than one-half hour. The 15,000-ton structure, which opened in early 2000, can seat as few as 5,000 people for a concert to as many as 36,500 fans for an American football game. • The moving block contains 9,200 seats, restrooms, concessions, and environment-control components, and is the largest of its kind in the world. The MB can move 231 feet (70 meters) across the arena floor in 20 minutes. Utilities to the MB are controlled via automatic air-conditioning and plumbing connection and cutoff and an electric cable reel system that lets out or takes in slack automatically as the block moves. • The design team was led by Nikken Sekkei Ltd, in association with Ellerbe Becket and Flack+Kurtz Consulting Engineers. Additional support was provided jointly by Taisei Construction, Mitsubishi Heavy Industries, and UDK.

THE FUTURE OF THE PUBLIC FACILITIES INDUSTRY

A measure of how successful public assembly facilities can be under the guidance of a contracted services management firm is the Colorado Springs World Arena. Built with 90 percent foundation funding and private donations, the 8,500-seat arena and adjacent dual-sheet ice rink was a success literally from the start. The nonprofit El Pomar Foundation, which spearheaded construction of the facility, brought in Global Spectrum (then known as Globe Facility Services) to manage the facility early in 1996. Within two years, the facility had turned an operating profit of $500,000, playing host to numerous sports, civic, and entertainment events, including Colorado College hockey, *Disney On Ice*, the country-rock group Alabama, high school graduations, state political conventions, and other events. In its first full year of operation, more than 650,000 people attended events at the Colorado Springs World Arena.

Name That Facility

Buying and selling naming rights is a 1990s trend that will likely continue well into the 21st century. In 1999, almost 50 corporations signed naming rights agreements in North America for major arenas and stadiums, agreeing to pay almost $1.4 billion in the process. In 2000, several individual naming rights deals for U.S. stadiums and arenas exceeded $100 million.

Selling rights has become one of the hottest methods for public assembly facility owners and managers to contribute to the bottom line. Naming rights can offset operational expenses by anywhere from $100,000 to $5 million per year.

But the purchase of naming rights benefits both sides of the equation. When the referee tossed up the ball for the start of the NBA championship on the first Wednesday in June 2000, several hundred million television viewers around the world likely took note that the game was being played at the STAPLES Center in Los Angeles. STAPLES, an aggressive entry into the cutthroat office supply market, gains television exposure through the STAPLES Center that would cost billions of dollars if purchased at commercial advertising rates.

The $116 million-over-20-years deal that puts STAPLES's name on the beautiful new arena in Los Angeles—also home of the NHL's Los Angeles Kings—is one of the better financial arrangements the company has made since it started selling copiers, fax machines, computers, and printers.

Branding—the marketing concept that American corporations utilize to get their names in front of as many American consumers as possible—drives much of the naming rights activities. Cinergy is one of the nation's largest electric and gas utilities, an outcome of the 1995 merger of Cincinnati-based Cincinnati Gas & Electric

City-owned U.S. Cellular Arena in Cedar Rapids, Iowa, is managed by Compass Facility Management, whose many services include market analysis for new construction, planning food and beverage systems, marketing support, and operations auditing.

Company and PSI Energy of Plainfield, Indiana. Cinergy can shore up its home base in the increasingly competitive world of electric utility deregulation by paying $6 million over five years to put its name on Cincinnati's Cinergy Field.

Dean Bonham, CEO of the Bonham Group, a Denver-based sports and entertainment marketing group, predicted recently that naming rights will continue to be a popular method for public

WOMEN'S BASKETBALL TEAM REWARDS FANS

As of June 2000, fans of the Women's National Basketball Association (WNBA) Cleveland Rockers can sign up on-line or at home games for free membership to the FANCARD.NET program. FANCARD.NET is a leading high-tech, interactive marketing program from Austin, Texas–based AIM Technologies. Each time members attend a Rockers home game at Cleveland's Gund Arena, they can swipe their ATM-type FANCARDs at any of several special kiosks scattered throughout the facility. They receive points for each game they attend. The points accumulate toward free food and drinks, team merchandise and tickets, and discounts from sponsors. In return, the team and its sponsors get marketing information about their customers. As of this writing, more than 70 teams and venues in all six major sports leagues participate in the FANCARD.NET program. The Rockers are the first professional U.S. women's sports team to join a fan loyalty program.

---

assembly facility managers and owners to pay down operating expenses. Bonham said that prices that seemed high just five years ago will look like a bargain five years in the future. Bonham said that corporate demand will create upside pressure on the price of naming rights, as will increasingly aggressive marketing of sponsorship benefits by owners and managers of public assembly facilities.

Not everyone everywhere will embrace the new names. When naming rights to San Francisco's venerable Candlestick Park—named for the point of land jutting out into San Francisco Bay upon which the stadium sits—were purchased by 3Com, a Silicon Valley networking solutions firm, one Bay Area sportswriter summed up the feeling of not a few San Francisco Giants' fans. "To me," he said, "it'll always be 'the stick.'"

ENVIRONMENTAL CONSIDERATIONS

Innovations in the public assembly facility business don't end with privatized management or naming rights. Environmental considerations are also taking center stage. It has been just over 30 years since a handful of college activists held the first Earth Day. But during those years, a new environmental ethic has taken hold in the world's consciousness. Public assembly facility managers have to take that environmental ethic into account when building or renovating facilities. Environmental awareness will become a fact of life for the public assembly facility industry in the 21st century.

The quadrennial gathering of the world's athletes is a valid case in point. Architects who planned Sydney's Olympic Stadium, which hosted the 2000 Summer Olympics, incorporated new environmental techniques into the design of the futuristic new arena. A "gray water" system recycles rainwater and water from lavatories, sinks, and dishwashers into the site's irrigation and fire suppression systems.

Energy-efficient and solar lighting illuminate the Olympic Stadium. "Green power" produced from water, wind, or solar resources provided the electricity for the Olympic games. Recyclables were separated out from the tons of trash generated by the two-week-long event. Architects installed specialized copper piping throughout the mammoth facility in order to avoid the use of polyvinyl chloride (PVC) piping and its threat to the ozone layer.

Public assembly facilities worldwide are incorporating energy efficient techniques and equipment.

In the northeastern United States, PSEG Energy Technologies offers 75-kilowatt turbogenerators to stadiums, arena-auditoriums, and other entertainment venues to reduce energy bills. Clean, quiet, environmentally friendly, and capable of being run on a number of fuel sources, the turbogenerators can be linked together to power large loads such as those created by public assembly facilities.

In Corpus Christi, Texas, the Bayfront Plaza Auditorium and Convention Center uses thermal energy storage to reduce peak energy demand charges. By using electric energy to chill water, ice, or eutectic salts during off-peak hours and storing that chilled medium in a tank, a facility such as the Bayfront Plaza can reduce its air-conditioning bill by thousands of dollars a month.

Energy efficiency is good for the environment and can contribute directly to the public assembly facility's bottom line.

What Else Is Coming?

Gazing into a crystal ball is never an easy task, but if the past is any guidepost to the future, then the outlook for the public assembly facility industry is a bright one indeed.

New and bigger stadiums, arenas, convention centers, amphitheaters, and performing arts centers are under construction or on the drawing boards. Existing convention centers are slated for major expansion and renovation projects that will add millions of square feet of convention center space in the first decade of the 21st century.

Plans are afoot to market entertainment and sporting events on the Internet by Webcasting sold-out events. Public assembly facilities, promoters, and ticketing companies will likely share revenues from Internet Webcastings, an industry (or sector) that is forecast to grow rapidly in the years ahead. Technology will play a major role in the design of new energy-efficient public assembly facilities, ranging from climate-controlled seating systems to modern fiber-optic communications networks for signage and lighting.

Concessions have changed dramatically in the past decade and will continue to evolve in the years ahead. Audiences will still be able to partake of hot dogs and popcorn, but ethnic and gourmet food at sporting and entertainment events will carve out a growing market share of concession sales. Exotic dishes such as salmon salad with balsamic vinaigrette dressing or lemon-grass chicken and oolong tea will increasingly become the stadium fare of choice for sports fans in the 21st century.

Facilities themselves are becoming more multidimensional than they were in the past. When the Conseco Fieldhouse opened in downtown Indianapolis in late 1999, it replaced Market Square Arena, just a few blocks away. It also vastly expanded the sports and entertainment options available to the residents of central Indiana.

The Fieldhouse is the home of the NBA's Indiana Pacers, but plays host to dozens of other sporting, entertainment, and community

THEMED ATTRACTIONS SUCH AS THE CLARIAN HEALTH PAVILION AT INDIANAPOLIS'S CONSECO FIELDHOUSE WILL BECOME MORE AND MORE A PART OF PUBLIC ASSEMBLY FACILITIES OF THE FUTURE. IN ADDITION TO CONCESSIONS, THE PAVILION OFFERS A LIFE-SIZE "OPERATION" GAME.

COMING ATTRACTIONS

events ranging from high school basketball tournaments to hockey games to concerts to the World Swimming Championships in 2004. In March 2000, the new facility hosted 26 events in 31 days. The building is designed to make changeovers quick and easy, and the facility's manager estimated that the facility would schedule between 200 and 250 events in 2000—more than double the number of events scheduled in a typical year at Market Square Arena.

Many stadiums and arenas are beginning to offer additional amenities and attractions that carry a sports theme, such as sports bars and/or kids areas with interactive games. According to Hellmuth, Obata and Kassabaum's David Greusel in his 1997 article, "The Coming Convergence," this marriage of sports and entertainment is blossoming, and is producing facilities that feature a "complete integration of sports and entertainment experiences that blends the reality and excitement of professional sports with the story line, interactivity, and attention to detail found in a well-run theme park." Currently, the themed sports facility has not yet completely arrived, but some stadiums are already on their way. These include the Pro Player Stadium in Miami, which is expanding its existing "NFL Experience" attraction, and Atlanta's Turner Field, which added some themed attractions following the 1996 Summer Olympics.

Finally, as in any industry, the human factor will continue to be the most important element in the public assembly facility business. As industry management has become more professional in the 1990s, it has also become more diverse, from a gender, ethnic, and racial standpoint. The International Association of Assembly Managers reflects the changes in the industry. A decade ago, IAAM's membership was just over 10 percent female. Today, the Association's female membership is pushing 20 percent, and that will likely grow as aging baby boomers retire from public assembly facility management.

The more things change, the more they remain the same. At the time of this writing, Cablevision Systems had plans to announce its decision to build a new Madison Square Garden on the site of the present Garden, atop Penn Station, or over the nearby railyards in west Manhattan. The present Garden is the fourth building so named in the institution's more than 125-year history, and millions of New Yorkers have flooded off the subway at 34th Street and Pennsylvania Station to take in a Knicks or Rangers game at the Garden.

Perhaps 30 years from now, a white-bearded patriarch in Queens will tell his great-grandchildren about going to see the Knicks play in the Garden. And they will know exactly what he is talking about.

Charles A. McElravy, who helped found the IAAM more than 75 years ago, would understand and approve.

The Expo Center at the Cumberland County Coliseum complex in Fayetteville, North Carolina, is used for banquets, exhibitions, meetings, and conventions. The 60,000-square-foot building can be divided into four sections of different sizes by movable, soundproof walls. An 8,000-square-foot hospitality area joins the center to the Crown Coliseum.

The Future of the Public Facilities Industry

SEVEN
CORPORATE PROFILES

PHOTO: © ROBERT GARVEY/CORBIS

FUTURE OF THE INDUSTRY

113

GLOBAL SPECTRUM

GLOBAL SPECTRUM PROVIDES INNOVATIVE, CUSTOM-DESIGNED FACILITY AND EVENT MANAGEMENT SERVICES FOR ARENAS, STADIUMS, CONVENTION CENTERS, AND THEATERS WORLDWIDE.

Global Spectrum provides innovative management and consulting solutions for the superior management, operation, support, and start-up of arenas, stadiums, convention centers, and theaters worldwide.

Global Spectrum was established in January 2000 after Philadelphia, Pennsylvania–based Comcast-Spectacor acquired a majority interest in Tampa, Florida–based Globe Facility Services (GFS). Founded in 1994, GFS attracted Comcast-Spectacor's interest in part because of the firm's unprecedented growth in recent years. Comcast-Spectacor, a subsidiary of the Comcast Corporation, owns and operates the First Union Center, First Union Spectrum, Philadelphia Flyers, Philadelphia 76ers, Philadelphia Phantoms, Flyers Skate Zone, and Comcast SportsNet. Through its affiliation with Comcast-Spectacor and its parent company, Comcast Corporation, Global Spectrum provides tremendous resources to all its facilities.

SHOWN HERE (FROM LEFT) ARE PETER LUUKKO, CHAIRMAN OF GLOBAL SPECTRUM AND PRESIDENT OF COMCAST-SPECTACOR VENTURES; MICH SAUERS, PRESIDENT AND CEO OF GLOBAL SPECTRUM; AND ED SNIDER, CHAIRMAN OF COMCAST-SPECTACOR.

THE GLOBAL SPECTRUM PERFORMANCE TEAM IS COMPOSED OF CORPORATE EXECUTIVES AND FACILITY GENERAL MANAGERS (GMS). SHOWN HERE (FROM LEFT) ARE DAVID NADEAU, HARBORVIEW CENTER GM; MIKE SCANLON, SOVEREIGN BANK ARENA ASSISTANT GM; TOM PAQUETTE, DIRECTOR OF EVENT PRODUCTION, FIRST UNION COMPLEX; BRIAN OHL, WHITTEMORE CENTER ARENA GM AND REGIONAL VICE PRESIDENT OF FACILITY MANAGEMENT; PETER LUUKKO, GLOBAL SPECTRUM CHAIRMAN; MICH SAUERS, GLOBAL SPECTRUM PRESIDENT AND CEO; DOT LISCHICK, COLORADO SPRINGS WORLD ARENA GM; GERRY BARON, MANAGER, SPECIAL PROJECTS; DEAN DENNIS, PUEBLO CONVENTION CENTER GM; AND JOHN PAGE, FIRST UNION COMPLEX GM AND REGIONAL VICE PRESIDENT OF FACILITY MANAGEMENT.

Global Spectrum strives to bring the finest events to the facilities it manages and to assist each facility owner in steadily increasing events, attendance, and revenues. Global Spectrum is committed to worldwide growth and leadership in the management of public assembly facilities and events.

The Global Spectrum executive staff is composed of highly skilled professionals with experience in all aspects of public assembly facility management. Teamwork is an important part of the company's success. Global Spectrum encourages its team members to communicate and share advice and information with their counterparts at other facilities. The company also prides itself on being a "Performance Team", with a focus on delivering results, not promises.

Since no two facilities, markets, or owners are identical, the Global Spectrum management philosophy is to tailor its services to meet and exceed the particular expectations of every client. Global Spectrum custom designs a unique management solution for each customer. Owners of public assembly facilities can choose between full or contract management services. Global Spectrum offers management solutions in finance and administration, sales and marketing, human resources, operations, and event services.

Global Spectrum operates with an entrepreneurial business philosophy. By adapting proven industry practices and instituting creative new procedures, Global Spectrum–managed facilities function at high levels of operational and fiscal responsibility. For more information, contact Mich Sauers at 813/289-3611 or visit the company's Web site at www.global-spectrum.com.

115

BIBLIOGRAPHY

Amusement Business. *2000 Audarena Stadium Guide and Facility Buyers Guide.* New York: BPI Communications, 1999.

———. *International Association of Auditorium Managers, 1925–1975: The First Fifty Years.* New York: BPI Communications, 1976.

Baugus, R.V. "But Will It Play in Biloxi?" *Facility Manager* (Winter 1991): 33.

Beck, Bill. *Indianapolis Convention & Visitors Association: 75 Years of Marketing Indianapolis.* Indianapolis, IN: Indianapolis Convention & Visitors Association, 1998.

Brubaker, Steve. "Turn of the Millennium Convention Centers," *Facility Manager* (November–December 1998): 7–10.

Byrnes, Charles. "The IAAM View." *Amusement Business* (February 14, 1970).

"Cool Idea Is Born in Sunny California." *Indianapolis Star,* December 25, 1999, p. C4.

Cunningham, Bill. "IAAM Districts and Organization." Memorandum to Carol Wallace. November 20, 1999.

Cunningham, Bill. "The Way We Were: A History of IAAM's Annual Conference and Trade Show." *Facility Manager* (July–August 1996).

Deckard, Linda. "The Buildings: Auds, Arenas, and Stadiums." *Amusement Business 100th Anniversary Special Edition* (November 1994): 126–131.

Dyja, Tom, project ed. *USA Today: The Complete Four Sport Stadium Guide.* New York: Fodor's Travel Publications, 1994.

Francis, Allison, and Lora Levosky. *Profile: The Convention Center Industry, The Supply Side of the Conventions, Expositions, and Meetings Market.* Philadelphia: Center City Group, Temple University, December 1999.

Greusel, David. "The Coming Convergence." *WCVM Journal* on-line (September 4, 1997). Available from www.venue.org/Journal2.htm.

Herrick, Julie. "The Challenges Facing the Future of Facility Managers." *Facility Manager* (September–October 1999): 26.

Herrick, Julie. "Dancing for Dollars: Can You Profit from Non-Profits?" *Facility Manager* (October–December 1993).

International Association of Assembly Managers. *1999 Guide: Members and Services Directory,* Irving, Tex.: IAAM, 1999.

International Association of Assembly Managers School for Public Assembly Facility Management. *In-House Promotion and Event Management.* PAFMS Monograph 113. Calgary, Alberta, Canada: 1997.

John, Geraint, and Rod Sheard. *Stadia: A Design and Development Guide.* Oxford: Butterworth Architecture, 1994.

Labinsky, Ronald J., and Doug Kingsbury. "Sports Stadia." *Encyclopedia of Architecture, Design, Engineering, and Construction.* New York: John Wiley and Sons, 1991.

"Live Shows Outearn Films, Sports." *Newsday,* September 18, 1998.

"Management by Teamwork." *Facility Manager* (July–August 1999).

McManamy, Rob. "Milwaukee Expresses Conventional Wisdom." *Design-Build* on-line magazine (April 1998). Available from www.designbuildmag.com/c498.asp.

Mooradian, Don. "Tunica Mississippi Arena and Exposition Center." *Amusement Business* (May 29, 2000): 13–16.

"Naming Rights." *Facility Manager* (July–August 1999): 43.

Parkinson, Tom. "Fifty Years Recounted, Anniversary Points to Future." *Auditorium News* (December 1974).

Peters, Steve. "Understanding the World of Private Management." *Facility Manager* (July–August 1999).

Peterson, David C. *Sports, Convention, and Entertainment Facilities.* Washington, D.C.: The Urban Land Institute, 1996.

Rippetoe, Rip. "A Different Point of View," *Facility Manager* (Fall 1990): 29.

Rundle, Rhonda L. "New Battlefield for E-Tickets: Home Printers." *Wall Street Journal,* February 17, 2000, p. B1.

Seitz, Robert. "Facing the Music." *Facility Manager* (May–June 1999).

Sword, Doug. "Economy Scores Big Win Thanks to Playoff Mania." *Indianapolis Star,* January 16, 2000, p. A1.

Tradeshow Week. *Tradeshow Week's Major Exhibit Hall Directory.* Twenty-second Annual Edition (August 1999).

Traiman, Steve. "New Construction Totals More than $4 Billion." *Spotlight-Concert Venues* (September 14, 1998): 45–47.

Vinson, Tammy. "SuiteHeart Deals." *Facility Manager* (March–April 1998).

Vivian, Jack, and Robert L. Dunn. "Ice Is Hot." *Facility Manager* (September–October 1999).

Waddell, Ray. "American Airlines Arena: The New Home to The Heat Promises To Be One Hot Place To Be." *Amusement Business* (January 17, 2000).

Waddell, Ray. "New Orleans Arena Fills Market Void." *Amusement Business* (October 25, 1999): 8.

Wharton, David. "Home Suite Home." *Los Angeles Times,* June 27, 1999, p. D1.

Williams, A'Lisha. "What's in a Name?" *Facility Manager* (January–February 1999).

Yaeger, Carl J. "Sydney 2000: The First 'Green' Olympics." *Facility Manager* (November–December 1998): 17–19.

Web sites: AIM Technologies; Aramark; Compass Facility Management; Conseco Fieldhouse; Corbis; Ellerbe Beckett; Event Software; Globe Facility Services; International Association of Assembly Managers; Kansas City Ballet; Leisure Management International; Los Angeles Philharmonic Association; Perceptual Robotics, Inc. (PRI); SMG; Spectacor Management Group; Tickets.com, Walt Disney Concert Hall; Will Rogers Memorial Coliseum; Wisconsin Center District.

INDEX

Admission Network, 87
Aim Technologies, 109
Alamodome, 84
Albuquerque, 41
Allen, Paul, 104
Allen County War Memorial Coliseum, 9
ALL-TEL Arena, 73, 104, 105
American Airlines, 73
AmericanAirlines Arena, 61, 73
American Seating Company, 84, 98
Americans with Disabilities Act, 83
America's Center, 61
Amphitheaters, 21
Amusement Business, 9
Anheuser-Busch Companies, Inc., 92–93
Ann Arbor, 41
ARAMARK, 105
Arena Club, 73
Arena Football League, 75
Arena Management conference, 15
Arenas, 18, 24, 25
Arison, Micky, 73
Astrodome, 22, 58, 85
AstroTurf, 85
Atlanta, 57, 59
Auditorium Managers Association (AMA), 4, 5, 8
Auditoriums, 18–19, 24, 25
Auditorium News, 8, 9
Australia, 11, 12, 21
Ballpark in Arlington, 22, 59
Ballparks, 21, 22, 24, 59
Baltimore, 22, 57, 86
Bank One Ballpark, 41, 59
Barnum & Bailey Circus, 9
Baseball, 38–39, 41
Bayfront Plaza Auditorium, 110
BC Place Stadium, 58
Beaver Stadium, 41, 76
Bennett, Tony, 36
Berlin, 11, 12
Bethesda, Md., 57
Bexar County, Tex., 25
Billboard, The, 8
Bonham, Dean, 108–09
Bonham Group, 70, 108
Boston, 39, 58, 59
Boston Garden, 41
Brazil, 19
Briggs Stadium, 41
Brookings, S. Dak., 84
Bryant-Denny Stadium, 76
Buck, Paul, 42
Budweiser, 86

Buffalo, N.Y., 9, 86
Bugge, William, 4
Burtness Center, 76
Busch, Adolphus, 86
Byrnes, Charles R., 9, 10, 74
California, 2, 41, 44, 77, 81, 83, 87
Candlestick Park, 109
Carnegie Hall, 84
Carter, Amon G., 18
Center for the Study of Crowd and Spectator Behavior, 12
Certificates of participation, 70
Certified facilities executive (CFE) program, 11
Charles A. McElravy Award, 10
Charlotte Auditorium, 42
Charlotte Coliseum, 41
Chemstrand, 85
Chicago, 2, 4, 10, 12, 39, 41, 43, 54–56, 58, 84, 104, 105
Chicago Amphitheater, 9
Chicago Cubs, 104
Chicago Stadium, 4
Christensen, Edna, 9
Cincinnati Reds, 38, 39
Cinergy, 70, 108
Cinergy Field, 39
Clarin, A Division of Greenwich Industries, L.P., 94
Clarin, Werner, 83
Clarity Visual Systems, 84
Clark Construction Group, 57
Cleveland, 4, 15, 22, 59
Cleveland Rockers, 109
Cobo Conference/Exhibition Center, 87
Colorado College, 108
Colorado River, 55
Colorado Springs World Arena, 105, 108
Colosseum, 16, 52
Columbia River, 55
Comerica Park, 84
Comiskey Park, 59, 84
Compaq, 71
Compaq Center, 71, 83
Compass Facility Management, 105, 107
Conference centers, 23
Congress centers, 23
Conseco, 70
Conseco Fieldhouse, 110–111
Convention and trade shows, 44
Convention centers, 23, 24–25, 44
Convention Liaison Committee, 10
Cook County, 55
Coors, 70

Coors Field, 22
Coppel, Tex., 15
Corey, Winifred, 9
Corpus Christi, Tex., 110
Cream City Associates, 57
Crosley Field, 38, 41
Crowd Management, 15
Crowd Management Seminar, 12
Cumberland County Coliseum Complex, 34
Daktronics Inc., 84, 90–91
Dallas, 18, 57
Dallas Convention Center, 33
Dallas–Fort Worth, 12
Dallas–Fort Worth International Airport, 15
Darrel K. Royal Memorial Stadium, 76
Deficit Reduction Act of 1984, 68
Denver, 22, 59, 70, 104, 105
Design-build, 55
Detroit, 2, 11, 36, 39, 58, 84, 87
Dickey, Lincoln, 4
Digital Menuboard, 84
Disney On Ice, 108
Dollywood, 59
Duluth, Minnesota, Convention and Civic Center, 36
Ebbetts Field, 41, 58
Elden, John, 11
Eli Lilly & Company, 71
Ellerbe Becker, 59, 107
El Paso Convention Center, 105
El Pomar Foundation, 108
Europe, 11, 22, 23
European Association of Arena and Auditorium Managers (EAAAM), 11, 15
Event Software's 3D Event Designer, 86
Exhibit halls, 22–23, 24–25, 44
Facility Manager, 12, 15
FANCARD.NET, 109
Fenway Park, 39, 58, 59
Festival Hall, 84
First Educational Exposition, 9
Flack+Kurtz Consulting Engineers, 107
Florida, 9, 44
Forbes Field, 41
Ford, Henry, 2
Fort Worth, 18, 57
Forum, The, 2
IV World Cup of Football, 19
Front Row Seating, 83
Funding public facilities, 68–77
Gehry, Frank, 21

Geiger Engineers, 64
Global Spectrum, 105, 108, 114
Globe Theatre, 38, 54
Great Depression, 4, 42, 58, 68
Green Bay, 41, 83
Gregory, Dixie, 8
Greusel, David, 59, 111
Grieb, Joseph G., 4
GSA Asia, Ltd., 105
Hall, Charles R., 4
Harlem Globetrotters, 9
Hartford Civic Center, 83
Hellmuth, Obata & Kassabaum (HOK), 58–59, 111
Henie, Sonja, 7
Highland Park, 2
High Tech/High Touch: the Co-Evolution of Technology and Culture, 39
HNTB, 59
Hofheinz, Judge Roy, 58
Holiday on Ice, 5, 41
Hollywood Bowl, 2, 36
Homasote Company, 66
Hoover Dam, 55
Hope, Bob, 9
Houston, Tex., 22, 58, 70–71, 83, 85
Hubert H. Humphrey Metrodome, 22, 58, 73
Huitt-Zollars Inc., 57
Hyatt Hotel chain, 105
IAAM Annual Conference & Trade Show, 9
IAAM College Internship Program, 12
IAAM Executive Development Series (EDS), 11
IAAM Foundation, 7, 11–12
IAAM News, 12
Ice Follies of 1939, 7
Ice hockey, 74–75
Indiana Convention Center, 71
Indiana Pacers, 110
Indianapolis, 22, 71, 74, 110
Indianapolis Colts, 74
Indianapolis 500, 84
International Association of Auditorium Managers (IAAM), 4, 7–12, 15, 24, 42, 74, 111
International Convention Center Conference, 15
International Crowd Management Conference, 15
Irving, Tex., 41
Irwin Seating Company, 84
Jack Kent Cooke Stadium, 104

Jacksonville Coliseum, 84
Jacobs Field, 22, 41, 59
Jerome Schottenstein Center, 76, 83, 105
Joe Louis Arena, 36
Kaiser, Henry J., 55
Kansas City, 4, 8, 59
KDKA, 2
Khrushchev, Nikita, 41
KI, 83
Knoxville, 41
Kohl Center, 76
Lambeau Field, 41
Lambrecht Construction, 57
Las Vegas, 44
Las Vegas Convention and Visitors Authority, 30–31
Lee County Sports Complex, 38
Leisure Management International (LMI), 105
Lilly Endowment, 71
Lloyd and Morgan, 58
Lombardi, Ernie, 38
London, 52, 84
Long Beach Arena, 104
Los Angeles Dodgers, 18
Los Angeles Kings, 108
Los Angeles Lakers, 25
Los Angeles Memorial Coliseum, 16, 18, 54, 59
Los Angeles Philharmonic, 21
Los Angeles Raiders, 18
Los Angeles Rams, 18
Louisiana State University, 76
Louisiana Superdome, 75, 104
Lucent Technologies, 61
Luxury suites, 73
Mack, Connie, 22
Madison Square Garden, 4, 59, 111
Mamet, David, 43
Maple Leaf Gardens, 42
Maracana Stadium, 19
Market Square Arena, 110, 111
McCormick, Frank, 38
McCormick Place, 54–55
McCormick Place Contractors, Inc. (McPC), 57
McElravy, Charles A., 4, 5, 7, 8, 9, 111
MCI Center, 105
Mc3D, 55, 57
Memphis Municipal Auditorium, 4, 5
Merchandise mart, 23
Metropolitan Pier and Exposition Authority (MPEA), 54–55
Miami, 61, 73, 105, 111
Miami-Dade County, 73

117

INDEX (CONTINUED)

Miami Heat, 61, 73
Michigan Stadium, 41
Microsoft, 104
Midwest Express Airlines, 71
Midwest Express Center, 57, 71
Mile High Stadium, 59, 104
Millennium Dome, 84
Miller Brewing Company, 28–29
Milwaukee, 4, 43, 57
Minneapolis, 4, 22, 58, 59, 73, 104
Mississippi, 75, 83
Missouri River, 55
Mitsubishi Heavy Industries, 107
Model T, 2
Molson Centre, 87
Monsanto, 85
Montreal, 2, 22, 87
Montreal Canadiens, 36, 42
Montreal Forum, 42
Myers, Don, 9
MyTickets, 87
Naisbitt, John, 39
Nashville Arena, 105
National Basketball Association (NBA), 24, 25, 61, 104
National Collegiate Athletic Association (NCAA), 22, 74
National Endowment for the Arts (NEA), 10, 23, 76
National Football League (NFL), 18, 22, 25, 104
National Highway Traffic Safety Administration, 12
National Hockey League (NHL), 25
National League (NL), 18, 24
NeoCon 99, 83
Nevada, 44
New Building Construction Board (NBCB), 8
New Orleans, 104
New Orleans Arena, 75
New Orleans Brass, 75
New Orleans Municipal Auditorium, 4
New York, 4, 39, 43, 58, 59, 77, 84, 85
New York Coliseum, 18
New York Yankees, 68
New Zealand, 11
Neyland Stadium, 41
Nikken Sekkei Ltd., 107
1936 Texas Centennial, 18
North Carolina, 42
Northern Kentucky Convention Center, 83
Norway, 104

Notre Dame Stadium, 41, 59
Oakland-Alameda County Coliseum, 59
Ogden Corporation, 105
Oglebay Resort and Conference Center, 7
Ohio Stadium, 41
Ohio State University, 41, 76, 83, 105
Olympic Games, 54, 87, 109, 111
Olympic Stadium, 22, 109
Ontario, Canada, 83
Oriole Park at Camden Yards, 22, 41, 57, 58–59, 86
Osaka, Japan, 84
Oslo Spektrum, 104
PAF managers, 44, 74, 80
Palm Springs Convention Center, 105
Parkinson, John, 54
Peace of Versailles, 2
Penn Station, 111
Pennsylvania State University, 41, 76
Perceptual Robotics (PRI), 83
Performing Arts Center of Los Angeles, 21
Performing Arts Committee, 10
Performing Arts Facility Administrators Seminar, 15
Peters, Steve, 107
Philadelphia, 39, 104, 105
Phoenix, 41, 59
Pico Group, 105
Pittsburgh, 2, 39, 104
Plan for a Living Archive, 12
P.M. Haeger and Associates, 10
Polo Grounds, 41, 85
Portland, Ore., 36, 84, 87, 104
Prague, Czech Republic, 19
Presley, Elvis, 42, 43
PriceWaterhouse-Coopers, 24
Professional Auditorium Management Symposium, 11
Professional Convention Management Association (PCMA), 25
Professional Development Committee, 7, 12
Progressive Architecture Magazine, 21
Pro Player Stadium, 105, 111
PSEG Energy Technologies, 109–110
Public assembly facility (PAF), 16
Public Facility Management School (PFMS), 7, 12
Public Works Administration (PWA), 18, 68
Radio City Music Hall, 84
Ralph Wilson Stadium, 86
Raymond James Stadium, 83

RCA, 70
RCA Dome, 22, 74
Redlands Stadium, 38
R.I.C. Corp., 99
Ringling Brothers, 9
Rio de Janeiro, 19
Riverfront Stadium, 38, 39
Robert T. Williams & Associates, 57
Romans, 16, 36, 38, 52
Roosevelt, President Franklin D., 18
Rose Bowl, 2, 41
Rose Garden, 36, 87, 104
Rupp Arena, 41
Ruppert, Col. Jacob, 2, 68
Ruth, Babe, 22, 68
Sadler Group, 57
SAFECO, 70
SAFECO Field, 41, 59, 61, 84
St. Louis, 61, 85
Saitama Super Arena, 59, 107
Salt Lake City, 87
San Antonio, 104
San Antonio Spurs, 25, 44
San Diego Convention Center Corporation, 35
Seattle, 41, 58, 59, 61, 84
Seattle Kingdome, 59
Shakespeare, William, 38, 54
Shouse, Louis, 4
Siren Technologies, 84
Six Companies, 55
SMG, 104–05
Smith, Bucklin & Associates, 10
Snyder, Daniel, 104
Society for the Preservation of Professional Touring Entertainment History, 12
Sokol, 19
Soldier Field, 2, 104
Soviet Union, 41
Springfield Civic Center, 83
Stadiums, 21–22, 24, 25, 41
STAPLES Center, 21, 25, 61, 68, 73, 83, 105, 108
State College, 41
Stephen C. O'Connell Center, University of Florida, 32
Stevens, Harry M., 85
Stockton, Calif., 59
Strahov Stadium, 19
Stutz, 2
Summer Olympics, 18
Sunmount Inc., 57
Super Bowl, 22

Swinburn, John, 12, 15
Sydney Opera House, 21, 52
Sylvan Industries Inc., 97
Syracuse Stage, 43
Taisei Construction, 107
Tampa Ice Palace, 104
Target Center, 73
Tax Reform Act of 1986, 68, 107
Techniques for Effective Alcohol Management (TEAM), 12
Tennessee River, 55
Terra-Mar, Inc., 57
Texas, 9, 15, 44
Texas International Raceway, 57
Texas Stadium, 41
Texas Tech University, 76
Thayer, Mert, 9
Theaters, 19, 21, 24
Thomas & Mack Center, 87
Thomas J. White Stadium, 105
Thompson Ventulett Stainback & Associates (TVS), 57
Thornton-Tomasetti Engineers, A Division of The Thornton-Tomasetti Group Inc., 65
3Com, 70, 109
Three Rivers Stadium, 104
Ticketmaster, 100
Ticketmaster.com, 87
Ticketmaster Online–City Search, 87
Tickets.com, 87, 95
Tiger Stadium, 58, 76
T.J. Lambrecht Construction, 57
Tokyo, 59, 107
Toledo, 41, 59
Toronto, 22, 42
Trade centers, 23
Trade fair, 22
Trade Show Weeks's 1999 Major Exhibit Hall Directory, 25
Trail Blazers, 36, 87, 104
Tribune Company, 102, 104
TrueLook system, 83
Tucson Convention Center, 83
Tulane University Green Wave, 75
Tunica Arena and Exposition Center, 75
Turner Field, 59, 83, 111
UDK, 107
United Center, 41
United Service Organizations (USO), 42
United Spirit Center, 76
United Supermarkets, 76
University of Alabama, 76
University of Illinois, Champaign, 11

University of Louisville, 12
University of Michigan, 41
University of Nebraska, 36
University of Nevada at Las Vegas (UNLV) Athletics, 87
University of North Dakota, 76
University of Southern California Trojans, 18
University of Tennessee, 41
University of Texas, 76
University of Wisconsin, 76
Utzon, Jorn, 52
Value City Arena, 76
Vancouver, B.C., 58
Venue Management Association (VMA), 15
Veterans Stadium, 105
Virco, 83
Walt Disney Concert Hall, 21
Walt Disney World, 59
Warneke, Heinz, 11
Warner Theatre, 2
Washington, D.C., 2, 105
Washington Redskins, 104
Web sites, 86–87
Wheeling, W. Va., 7
White Plains, N.Y., 12
White Way Sign Company, 84, 96
Will Rogers Coliseum, 18
Wilson, Morris, Crain and Anderson, 58
Windsor, Ontario, 11
Wisconsin Center District, 71
WLS radio, 43
Women's Basketball Association (WNBA), 109
Woodstock, 43
Works Progress Administration (WPA), 4, 9, 68
World Council for Venue Management (WCVM), 15
World Swimming Championships, 111
World War I, 2
World War II, 8, 58, 68
World Wrestling Federation Entertainment, Inc., 48–50
Wrigley Field, 21, 39, 41, 58, 84, 104, 105
Xcel Energy, 70
Yale Bowl, 21
Yankee Stadium, 2, 21, 58, 68, 83
Zamboni, Frank, 80-81
Zambonis, 81